by

Martha Langdon-Dahm, Ph. D.

Pat J

TRADE SECRETS ™

25

Proven

Success

Tools

for

Working

Dealing

and Winning

with

People

LEARNING DEVELOPMENT SYSTEMS, INC.
PUBLISHERS
DAYTON, OHIO

TRADE SECRETS
by Martha Langdon-Dahm, Ph.D.

Copyright© 1986 by Martha Langdon–Dahm, Ph.D.
Published by Learning Development Systems, Inc.
Printed in the United States of America

Cover Designer: Mark Riedy

Library of Congress Catalog Card Number: 85-82343

ISBN 0-936585-00-5

CONTENTS

SECTION I
25 Proven Success Tools

SECTION II
25 Reinforcement Cards

This Section contains a built-in Tool
Kit. The Kit consists of twenty-five
Reinforcement Cards. These Cards are
found in the back of this book.

QUICK REFERENCE TABLE

SOME TYPICAL SITUATIONS

INTRODUCTION

That's a **Trade Secret!** You've used that expression many times — haven't you? Now ask yourself, "What does that expression really mean?" And, can you remember one of your trade secrets? While you are thinking of your answers, here are a few secrets I have heard from professionals like yourself.

Successful real estate agents have at least one trade secret. It's the approach they use to make every *"Open House"* positively pay off for themselves and their sellers.

A dentist friend of mine revealed one of his trade secrets. He motivates his patients to invest in their mouths. As he says, *"I get them to put their money where their mouths are!"*

There are managers who know that a real open-door policy only works well with open-minded employees, since close-minded employees tend to shut doors behind them. And, most successful salespeople use this trade secret: "First, you sell yourself and then, you sell your product to your customer." Many secretaries, who have joined the computer age, have acquired another trade secret. They use *word processors* and their work output is simpler, more effective and more efficient. Just watch them!

In sports, football players understand that it isn't the player who first carries the ball, but the one who holds the ball at the end of the play that matters. Successful players quickly learn this trade secret.

Here are a few trade secrets from educators and parents. Educators, who are interested in teaching students ways of thinking rather than what to think, realize that learning is *discovering questions to other peoples' answers.* Certainly, a proven success tool of their trade! Wise parents are aware of a trade secret for raising healthy children. These parents recognize and own their problems instead of blaming and projecting these problems on their children.

So, from my inside sources, you have become privy to other professionals' trade secrets. Generally speaking, **TRADE SECRETS ARE BELIEFS, METHODS, APPROACHES, FORMULAS, TECHNIQUES OR TOOLS THAT PEOPLE USE IN THEIR PROFESSION OR TRADE FOR POSITIVE PAYOFFS.** Because most of us rarely share any of our secrets, professionals rarely share their trade secrets.

There are twenty-five **TRADE SECRETS** in this book. These proven success tools will help you achieve success with all kinds of people in various situations. These tools work in situations involving group meetings or one-to-one appointments.

I'm sharing these **TRADE SECRETS** with you, the reader, because under close scrutiny, you have proven your ability to keep confidences, follow instructions and properly use specific tools to achieve specific results. But these tools need to be handled with great care for precautionary purposes.

Let's talk about a tool that's familiar to most of you, *"Name Calling."* Why would a person need to use this tool? Well, one reason, it's a valuable asset to have and to use when you need to get a particular person's full attention. How would a person gain expertise in the use of this tool? One way is to practice using the tool. But, you and I both know some people who would be uncomfortable hearing their name used repeatedly in a specific situation by the same speaker. So, I recommend cautious use of this tool. Realize, too, that there is more to this tool than meets the eye. Remember, I am sharing **TRADE SECRETS** with you and this is one of them. If you want, turn immediately to page 121 and read from an inside source how you can use this important *"Name Calling"* tool with expertise.

Whether you are currently using the tool, *"Name Calling"* or not, there are other tools you may be using on a daily basis. Some of you have already considered these personal tools to be your *trade secrets*. Why? Because your tools have helped you survive in situations involving yourselves and other people. So, you do have a set of tools that you do use, whether you are aware of them or not.

With your tools in mind, think about one of your typical days. Which tool did you use to convince someone that her way of thinking was not the only way to think? Or, how did you get a person to "open up" to you? Which tool did you use to cope with your supervisor's remarks which told you little or nothing about what you really needed to know? When someone brought you a problem, which tool did you immediately use to manage or resolve it? Tough questions? Certainly!

When you think about it, most of us use a certain tool because it's familiar, it's available and it's reliable. These are good criteria. However, there are better criteria to apply when selecting the best tool for a specific situation.

In **TRADE SECRETS**, the twenty-five tools have been selected for their proven success record. These tools will work only if you use them properly. They will become your **TRADE SECRETS** only if you become familiar with them and gain expertise in using them. As with any product of high quality, these tools are "finely tuned" to work best under specified conditions. The tools become "user friendly" when you acquaint yourself with their conditions described in each tool. The general format will explain each of these conditions.

EXPLANATION OF FORMAT

TITLE

Each tool has a specific name. This name will be located at the top of the page introducing the tool.

DEFINITION

There is a concise definition for each tool. This definition provides the user with guidelines for matching the right tool with the right need.

HOW THIS TOOL WORKS

To work the tool, you need to know which procedures to follow and, at times, which words to say. Each step begins with an action word implying that the user *actually* works the tool. Don't skip a step unless a particular step is marked "Option Step." Otherwise, follow each step.

SITUATIONS FOR USING THIS TOOL

This section includes suggestions of specific times, places and events to help you determine whether or not you need to use a particular tool. It is beneficial to use a specific tool to satisfy a specific need. As you become expert in handling these tools, you won't need to rely on this section for help. However, until this level of expertise has been reached, continue to refer to this section.

BENEFITS AND PAYOFFS

Each tool is carefully designed, field-tested and finely tuned to give you knowledge, applications and positive payoffs which you and others receive when you use each tool properly and expertly.

EXAMPLES OF PEOPLE USING THIS TOOL

Seeing is believing! This section helps you to "see" the tool in use and to "watch" how a person puts the steps into action. By reading each case in point, you get an inside look at the tool through the "eyes" of an expert.

CAUTION

This section begins with a typical caution word, "DON'T" followed by a reason why the user should follow this advice. Please recognize and follow the basic safety precautions before attempting to use any tool. This section ends with a friendly reminder to "DO" a specific action.

TROUBLESHOOTING

This section covers the basic procedures for checking the main sources of trouble when the tool does not operate properly for you or others.

A typical user, like yourself, might make the following comment: *"I'm using this tool and it doesn't seem to work for me."* When this situation occurs to you, turn to this section and reflect on probable sources of the problem.

Under the caption, NATURE OF DIFFICULTY, a user explains his or her problem in detail. Under the caption, SUGGESTIONS, the user receives two or more recommendations for correcting the problem. At times, additional references to other tools are given as cross reference material.

Due to the nature of some of the twenty-five tools, this section, **TROUBLESHOOTING**, may contain more than one problem for study purposes. When this situation occurs, know that each problem will include specific recommendations for managing or resolving the situation.

NOTE
This final section calls your attention to an important point regarding the use of this specific tool. At this time, you are in possession of a **TRADE SECRET.**

PRIOR TO OPERATION

When you begin to use any one of these tools, the steps may be difficult to recall because of your limited experience in using them. So, for your information, in the back of the book, there is a section containing **REINFORCEMENT CARDS.** This section includes twenty-five tool cards which may be torn out and set on your desk, in your car, in your hand, or in any place you want to put them. Each card contains essential steps for using a specific tool. These cards are your "support systems" until you become proficient in using the tools.

You're about to become acquainted with twenty-five **TRADE SECRETS.** Success-oriented people, like yourself, use these tools. So, prove to yourself that you are a success-oriented person! Begin to use these tools — use them properly — use them frequently. Then, the tools will become your **TRADE SECRETS!**

Section I

25 PROVEN SUCCESS TOOLS

TOOL 1

ACTIVE LISTENING

DEFINITION:

A TOOL WHICH ENABLES A LISTENER TO "TUNE IN" AND GRASP THE FEELINGS AND FACTS OF WHAT THE SPEAKER IS SAYING SO THAT THE SPEAKER FEELS UNDERSTOOD AND VALUED. ACTIVE LISTENING IS REFLECTIVE LISTENING.

HOW THIS TOOL WORKS:

1. Listen to the speaker's message to determine if this situation requires vou to do a special kind of listening called active listening.

   HERE ARE SOME INDICATORS:

   a. Speaker sends a problem-oriented message.

   "I'd like you to listen to this problem I'm having. Perhaps, if I could talk it out, it would help me."

   b. Speaker sends a strong feeling message.

   "I hate work."

   c. Speaker asks questions to hide true feelings.

   "When are we going to leave?"

   or

   "What do I have to do to get a raise around here?"

1

2. Show the speaker you are ready to actively listen.

HERE'S HOW:

a. Keep good eye contact.

b. Be comfortable with the giving of your time.

c. Verbalize and accept the feelings of the speaker. Start with *"You"* followed by a feeling word.

   "You feel angry. Right?"

d. Accept the fact that the speaker's feelings may change as you actively listen.

e. Have a sincere desire to help the person even if you only act as a "sounding board."

3. Tune in to the speaker's message and use *feeling words* which accurately reflect how the speaker feels.

HERE'S AN EXAMPLE:

Customer: *"I can't believe the treatment they give people around here!"*

You: *"You're upset about the lack of basic courtesies in some of the sales people, is that it?"*

Customer: *"Yes. For some reason, they think they're better than us."*

(Active listening occurs when the speaker verifies what you have said.)

4. Be careful not to evaluate or give your opinion on what is being said. Simply reflect the speaker's feelings and facts.

HERE'S HOW:

Speaker: *"I have a problem with the way he's painting the room."*

You: *"Sounds like you're not satisfied with the job he's doing."*

5. Actively listen as long as the speaker appears to want it. Usually, the speaker will give you a clue when it's time to stop or take another approach.

Some typical clues telling you to stop:

a. Speaker become silent.
b. Speaker begins fidgeting with paper, watch, etc.
c. Speaker gets up to go!
d. Speaker asks a direct question.
e. Speaker makes one of the following comments:
   — *"Well, thanks for listening."*
   — *"We're not getting anywhere."*

SITUATIONS:

- Responding to an opinionated statement of someone.
- Seeking to improve customer relations by listening to your customer complaints.
- Dealing with children who "mask" their feelings by asking questions.
- Facilitating coaching and counseling sessions; these sessions give people a chance to release their negative feelings.
- Selling situations: most people buy on their emotions rather than on their needs. So, focus on their feelings.
- Handling a person who resists changes of any kind.
- Acting as a change agent or "sounding board" for two people in conflict.

BENEFITS AND PAYOFFS:

1. Encourages you to do less talking and more listening.
2. Saves you time and prevents costly personnel problems by having you listen to peoples' concerns before they get "out of hand."

3. Helps you develop your ability to listen and understand. Often, people want to be understood by the other before they have taken time to understand the other.

    (This type of listening is nonevaluative and it's one of the most powerful agents for bringing about a change in another's personality.)

4. Calms people who get upset and allows them some time to express themselves when they need to. Active listening helps some people "settle down."

5. Provides opportunities for people to develop emotional maturity by helping them become more articulate in expressing their feelings and more accepting of constructive criticism.

6. Establishes an open, free environment for children and adults to share their feelings without being judged for having those feelings.

7. Contributes to your "weight loss" program since genuine listening is an active function which can increase your heart rate, shorten your breathing cycles and literally burn up your unwanted calories!

EXAMPLES OF PEOPLE USING THIS TOOL:

FAMILY SETTING

Husband: *"I just can't understand why you didn't get the oil changed in the car today. So, you were busy. We all were! You said you'd take care of it."*

Wife: *"You're frustrated with the way I handled my time today, right?"*

Husband: *"Sort of."*

(She accurately reflects his feeling.)

"We really shouldn't be driving that car any more. It needs fixing."

Wife: *"You're fearing that driving the car could really do more harm than good. That's what's bothering you."*

Husband: *"Yeah."*

(She accurately reflects his feeling again.)

"Did you make another appointment?"

Wife: *"I've got one at 8:00 a.m. tomorrow."*

(She answers his question without using active listening. She knows when to stop using this type of listening. See Step #5-d in HOW THIS TOOL WORKS Section.)

Husband: *"Great!"*

CAUTION:

DON'T use active listening when it is not needed! Not all listening situations require it. And, don't manipulate people into thinking your way by using active listening with them.

Reason: Some people have to be in the "right frame of mind" to have someone actively listen to them. Usually a person will send you a clue which says:

"Just listen to me. Don't try to solve my problem. Just let me bend your ear for awhile."

There are times when people ask you for directions or information. Using active listening in such situations would be inappropriate.

There are other times when people feel manipulated by someone's attempt to actively listen to them. These people feel you are "playing word games" or using "armchair psychology" on them and they resent your behavior.

DO use active listening in appropriate situations. Stay in a reflective mode and respond to their needs with "You-messages" that are properly worded. Remember, as a mirror reflects a variety of poses of the person in front of it, so can you reflect a variety of feelings and facts of people you are seeing and hearing as they share their concerns with you.

TROUBLESHOOTING:

"I'm using this tool and it doesn't seem to work for me."

NATURE OF DIFFICULTY — Problem

"I'm a new manager. One of my employees was in the cafeteria during break. He asked if he could join me at the table. I asked him how things were going. He responded with, 'You feel I'm upset and that's why I wanted to join you for coffee, right?' Now, for a minute, he had me confused! He was doing active listening on me. He was putting words in my mouth and he seemed defensive. So, I answered him, 'No.' How should I have handled his comment?"

SUGGESTIONS:

A. Be aware of the fact that a person can actively listen at any time. Know too, that this Tool is often misused. In your case, Jack was misusing this Tool.

(Jack went beyond the content of your message when he thought your reason for asking him to join you was because he was upset.)

In the future, you could respond to inaccurate messages by saying:

"Jack, when I ask you how things are going, I don't assume you're always going to give me a bad report. Besides, you can join me for coffee without bringing up work-related topics."

(You are being assertive because you are sharing your thoughts and feelings on the matter.)

B. Realize that some people actively listen without ever having been formally trained in the proper use of the Tool. They misuse the Tool! Yet, they still use it. That's a common problem with Tools!

NATURE OF DIFFICULTY — Problem

"I think active listening can be risky business! I run the risk of having my ideas changed when I listen, so intently, to someone else's ideas. So, what do I need to know if I want to do more active listening?"

SUGGESTIONS:

A. Be willing to "run the risk" of having your ideas changed! You are simply opening yourself to the other's experience and this is a choice you make.

B. Realize that a *defensive* person rarely does this type of listening, but a *flexible* person takes risks and actively listens when a situation presents itself.

NOTE:

HEARING IS A NATURAL, PHYSICAL FUNCTION OF THE EAR!

LISTENING IS AN INTELLECTUAL FUNCTION WHICH REQUIRES CARE, EFFORT AND TIME.

ACTIVE LISTENING IS AN INTELLECTUAL AND EMOTIONAL FUNCTION OF THE BODY-MIND WHICH REQUIRES THE LISTENER TO RESPOND TO THE FACTS AND FEELINGS OF THE SPEAKER. TO KNOW HOW AND WHEN TO USE THIS TYPE OF LISTENING IS A **TRADE SECRET.**

TOOL 2

ASKING OPEN-ENDED QUESTIONS

DEFINITION:

A TOOL FOR GETTING MORE INFORMATION, GREATER CLARITY, SPECIFIC DETAILS OR DIRECT ANSWERS FROM SPEAKERS. LISTENERS AND SPEAKERS USE THIS TOOL WHEN THEY WANT THE OTHER PERSON'S HONEST OPINIONS, FURTHER CLARIFICATIONS OR PRECISE ANSWERS ON AN ISSUE.

HOW THIS TOOL WORKS:

1. Listen to the statement or answer.

2. Ask questions that begin with stem words such as: "What," "Why," "When," "How," "Where," "In what way," "Tell me," "Describe for me . . ."

3. Choose one of these additional stem words: "Do," "Does," "Did," "Is," "Are," "Was," "Can," "Will," when you need a direct *"Yes"* or *"No"* answer.

    Judy: *"Did you put the keys back in the drawer?"*

    Pat: *"No, not yet."*

4. Ask "You-oriented" questions. There are two versions.

    Question format at the beginning:

    "What suggestions can you make?"

    Question format at the end:

    "You feel we can improve in this area. What suggestions can you make?"

5. Attach the person's name at the beginning of your question or at the end.

   "Bill, what suggestions can you make?"

   or

   "What suggestions can you make, Bill?"

6. Use a positive "up-beat" tone. There are many ways to say,

   "Why do you ask?"

7. Be sensitive and give full attention to the speaker by keeping your eyes focused on his or her eyes. Remember, no staring allowed.

SITUATIONS:

- Needing to prevent misunderstandings and short-comings in verbal and written communications.
- Planning and developing a format for performance appraisals and job interviews.
- Conducting the performance appraisal session or interview session.
- Checking one's understanding of another person's statement. Often, some people assume that what is said is always identical to what is meant.
- Gaining additional insight into a specific comment.
- Dealing with complaints and grievances.
- Wanting to show interest and genuine concern for the other person's feelings, views and attitudes.

BENEFITS AND PAYOFFS:

1. Demonstrates a constructive conversation skill for building understanding between people.

2. Gives the listener an opportunity to gain a deeper level of meaning when the statement sounds incomplete.

3. Promotes the sharing of complete information.

4. Increases a person's chances of receiving clear messages which saves time, effort and money at the front-end.

5. Enables a person to become a more objective thinker and listener. No longer is there a need to make hasty decisions with insufficient data.

6. Provides a needed channel for all parties to be understood. Open-ended Questions eliminate the need for assumption making.

EXAMPLES OF PEOPLE USING THIS TOOL:

SOCIAL SETTING

After dinner one evening, a group of parents is having a discussion on the proposed mill levy for their local school system.

Joe: *"I feel there's not even a glimmer of a chance this tax levy will pass."*

Jerry: *"What makes you feel so strongly that it'll be defeated, Joe?"*
(Open-ended Question)

Joe: *"Well, there's an anti-tax feeling among a number of community people and they don't believe the statistical data coming out of the administrative office."*

Jerry: *"I'm not clear on your last point, Joe. Why don't they believe the data?"*
(Open-ended Question)

* * *

11

BUSINESS SETTING

Customer: *"This appliance is defective and I'd like to replace it."*

Salesperson: *"I'd be glad to replace it. What happened when you tried to use it?"*
(Open-ended Question)

* * *

BUSINESS SETTING

Supervisor is developing a format of questions for her interview sessions with candidates.

— *What expectations do you have for this job?*

— *If you were to join our department, how would you contribute to our team building effort?*

— *Do you have one year goals and five year goals? If so, what are they?*

CAUTION:

DON'T psychoanalyze a person by asking too many Open-ended Questions at one time. For instance, some people ask a steady stream of questions, forgetting that they are carrying on a conversation — not an interview. During a conversation, it is not a good idea to ask a series of questions of a person.

Reason: Some people get the feeling they are being "tried" in a court or interrogated for wrong doing. They feel threatened and they begin to show defensive behaviors.

DO ask Open-ended Questions in a conversation when you need more clarity to adequately understand what the person is saying. Also, there are times when you need to ask the direct question. Ask it! "When in doubt — ask!"

TROUBLESHOOTING:

"I'm using this tool and it doesn't seem to work for me."

NATURE OF DIFFICULTY — Problem

"My boss asks Open-ended Questions but he doesn't seem to listen to my answers. What should I do?"

SUGGESTIONS:

A. Before responding to his first question, restate his question for his benefit.

"So, Mr. Becker, you would like to know how I see the project's time line. Right?"

(You are checking his listening before beginning your answer.)

B. After answering your boss's question, ask him this question in a respectful tone:

"What do you hear me saying, Mr. Becker?"

(You are checking his listening after answering his question.)

NATURE OF DIFFICULTY — Problem

"I hold weekly staff meetings. When I have covered all agenda items, I usually say to the staff, 'Any questions?' You see, I'm trying to stimulate some discussion among them. Well, it's not working! My staff doesn't seem to want to discuss anything. What do you suggest?"

SUGGESTIONS:

A. Ask Open-ended Questions and direct them to specific staff members.

An Example

"Doris, what are some positive points you received from today's meeting?"

(This approach will take some practice on your part. However, I guarantee that you will have some healthy interactions during your meetings.)

B. Allow other staff members to add their comments to the above question. Then, you may want to summarize their comments when all members have had an opportunity to speak.

Option: Write individual comments on the board. (This legitimizes the fact that you have listened to them and you have found their comments helpful.)

NOTE: DEVELOP EXPERTISE IN USING THE STEM WORDS LISTED IN STEPS #2 AND #3. THEN, MODIFY YOUR LIST TO FIT YOUR NEED. KNOWING HOW AND WHEN TO ASK OPEN-ENDED QUESTIONS IS A **TRADE SECRET.**

TOOL 3

BEING ASSERTIVE AND PROACTIVE

DEFINITION:

A TOOL WHICH HELPS YOU TELL OTHERS YOUR VIEWS, YOUR BELIEFS, YOUR NEEDS OR YOUR WAY OF DOING THINGS. IN THESE SITUATIONS, YOU ARE TACTFUL, FIRM AND RESPECTFUL OF THE RIGHTS OF OTHERS.

HOW THIS TOOL WORKS:

1. Assess your situation in terms of getting your wants and needs met. Be mindful of not deliberately violating the rights of the other. Here are examples of a person's rights:

   a. To express one's opinion.

   b. To judge one's own behavior.

   c. To change one's mind.

   Here are examples of a person who violates another person's rights:

   a. *"You don't know what you're talking about."*
      (An unfair criticism of another's opinion.)

   b. *"You can't do anything right."*
      (A *put down* to another person.)

   c. *"That won't work!"*
      (A person who speaks in *absolutes* or *God-like talk.*)

2. Decide what you specifically need to accomplish.
   "I need to tell Paul that I think he is misinformed about the exact amount of the bill."

3. Select words and phrases reflecting an assertive approach rather than an aggressive approach.

Assertive Phrases

"I need . . ."

"I don't understand . . ."

"I prefer . . ."

"I'm uncomfortable . . ."

Assertive speakers use "I-messages" and own their needs and feelings.

Aggressive Phrases

"You don't need . . ."

"You're an idiot."

"You're not doing it right."

Aggressive speakers use "You-messages" and speak in absolutes. They rarely own their needs or feelings. Why should they when they believe that they're always right!

4. Speak up or write down your thoughts in an assertive manner.

   "I thought you were going to have that task done by 2:00 today. I see it's not completed. What happened?"

   (Your tone is tactful.)

5. **Option Step:** Use behavioral rehearsal techniques to visualize yourself speaking or acting assertively. (See VISUALIZING TOOL, page 171.)

6. Realize that some people will view your assertive behavior as aggressive or "lacking tact." In such cases, you may want to adopt this motto:

Motto:

An honest expression of self without *intentionally* violating the other's rights.

SITUATIONS:

- Expressing your opinion in a threatening situation.
- Speaking up when someone has indicted you for something you didn't do. (When you do this, you are using an assertive tool called *Self Disclosure.*)
- Confronting an employee who is violating a company policy. (In the past, you may have used non-assertive behavior by avoiding the issue and hoping it would go away.)
- Telling your boss that you deserve a raise while presenting your rationale for the raise.
- Saying, *"I don't know,"* or *"I don't understand,"* when you honestly don't!
- Asking the chairperson for an ending time on a meeting. (In this instance, the start-up time was the only time given.)
- Taking an assertive stand when someone says, *"Do you mind if I smoke?"*
- Returning a defective piece of merchandise.
- Handling a phone caller who has called during your meal.
- Confronting a family member on a difficult issue.

BENEFITS AND PAYOFFS:

1. Allows you to express your feelings, needs and goals to others when you choose.

2. Gives you the freedom to say what you want and to feel confident and competent in your approach.

3. Teaches you how to eliminate conditioned and long-term negative behaviors. (An example of such behavior:)

   "I can't speak in groups because I've always been shy."

   By using assertive talk, you can choose to remain shy or to change your behavior. Now, it's up to you.

17

4. Allows you to socialize actively rather than passively.

5. Provides you with a "formula" to control certain personal behaviors which you know "turn people off."

6. Communicates to other people that you are a person of power and influence.

7. Empowers you to handle any situation while keeping you mindful of possible consequences.

8. Gives you the freedom to express your convictions tactfully.

9. Makes your life worth living!

EXAMPLES OF PEOPLE USING THIS TOOL:

Assertive Words	Aggressive Words	Non-Assertive Words
"I need . . ."	*"You should . . ."*	*"I don't know,"* (when I do).
"I would like . . ."	*"This is the only way . . ."*	*"I'm sorry,"* (when I don't mean it).
"No, I won't be able to . . ."	*"You didn't tell me to do that."*	*"It doesn't matter,"* (when it does).

* * *

SOCIAL SETTING: Restaurant Seating

Upon entering a restaurant, the hostess escorts your companion and you to a booth and turns and says, *"Is this all right?"*

Since it's close to the kitchen entrance, you respond, *"No, I'd prefer another booth please."*

(You do not have to give her your reason.)

* * *

18

BUSINESS SETTING: Delegating With Tact

Your manager has asked you to head up a special project which requires giving orders to co-workers and superiors. You want to do the job well. Rather than appearing pushy, you say to project members,

"I need your cooperation and work effort on this project. I know you can be resourceful to our entire project and I'll need to count on you for support."

(You are being honest and direct with them.)

* * *

BUSINESS SETTING: Handling Rumors and Gossip

One of your co-workers begins to tell you some gossip and you don't want to listen. You interrupt him and say,

"I'd prefer that you not tell me about that."

(You do not need to give him any reason. If you choose to give a reason — go ahead. If he continues telling you more, simply repeat your first response — over and over — until it "sinks in." When you use this approach, the assertive tool is called *Broken Record.*

CAUTION:

DON'T allow yourself to use self-limiting behaviors! Here are three types:

— Using Qualifying Expressions

"Maybe this is just my opinion, but . . ."

"I'm sorry to take so much of your time, but . . ."

— Speaking in Low Tones — using a whispered monotone because you do not value your own ideas and you think that no one else will either.

— Passive Listening — using no eye contact, making no comments and having no desire to become actively involved in a conversation or discussion.

Reason: Self-limiting behaviors tend to reduce the range of personal potential and personal choice available to people. Whether these behaviors show in peoples' body language, speech patterns or group interactions, these people are usually seen as nonassertive. They become "open targets" for aggressive people to manipulate and use to their advantage.

DO begin to realize that self-limiting behavioral patterns are acquired through long periods of conditioning with satisfying payoffs. Many people choose to continue using their self-limiting behavioral patterns because of the results/payoffs they receive — even if these payoffs are negative!

— Use Assertive Expressions

  "My opinion is . . ."

  "I need to take some of your time to . . ."

— Use a Well Modulated Tone

  "I'm proud of my voice and I speak to let others know what I think."

— Use Active Listening — (See ACTIVE LISTENING TOOL, page 1, and EYE POWER TOOL, page 73.)

TROUBLESHOOTING:

"I'm using this tool and it doesn't seem to work for me."

NATURE OF DIFFICULTY — Problem

"My supervisor seems to enjoy speaking negatively about certain members on our staff. He makes these comments to me. I really do not appreciate listening to them. The other day, when he started, I asserted myself and said to him, 'Sir, I prefer that you not tell me about your negative feelings toward members on our staff.' Well, he acted as if he didn't hear me and continued on with his gossip. So, what good does it do to speak assertively?"

SUGGESTIONS:

A. Use the *Broken Record* technique. Repeat your same assertive statement to him while he is telling you his gossip.

   "Sir, I prefer that you not tell me about your negative feelings toward members on our staff."

   (Don't "let up" until he hears you. Then, decide if you want to say more! Remember, do not change your original statement until he hears you.)

B. Use risk-taking behavior. Say to him:

   "Sir, I have work to do for you which is of a higher priority than what is taking my time now. So, I am leaving your office to go and do it. I know you want me to spend my work time in the most productive manner. Thank you for understanding and supporting me in this decision."

   (To do this, you may have to interrupt him. It is your right. It is also your option to exercise your right.)

C. Rehearse some of these statements to yourself either by writing them down and rereading them, or saying them in front of a mirror, while visualizing yourself saying these same words to your supervisor. (See VISUALIZING TOOL, page 171.)

NATURE OF DIFFICULTY — Problem

"Our director uses aggressive expressions when he talks to us on routine matters. We've begun to make derogatory remarks about him to each other. We need help!"

SUGGESTIONS:

A. First, you can ask clarifying questions of your director to see why he's making these aggressive comments toward the staff.

B. Second, you can give constructive feedback to each other when you hear a derogatory remark. (See GIVING FEEDBACK TOOL, page 87.)

NOTE: IT IS IMPORTANT TO KNOW THAT ASSERTIVE PEOPLE ARE PROACTIVE IN THEIR WORK. THEY ARE DECISIVE, HONEST LISTENERS WHO ACCEPT WORKABLE OUTCOMES. AT ANY TIME, THEY CAN CHOOSE TO BE ASSERTIVE OR NOT TO BE ASSERTIVE. THEY HAVE TOOLS TO HANDLE ANY SITUATION. THAT'S THEIR **TRADE SECRET!**

TOOL 4

BUILDING POSITIVE MORALE

DEFINITION:

> A TOOL FOR HELPING PEOPLE IMPROVE THEIR ENVIRON-
> MENT BY ENCOURAGING THEM TO USE, ON A CONSISTENT
> BASIS, CERTAIN TOOLS OF THEIR TRADE WHICH TEND
> TO PROMOTE GREATER PRODUCTIVITY. GREATER PRO-
> DUCTIVITY MEANS BETTERING PEOPLE INTERACTIONS
> AND REALIGNING THEIR WORKING CONDITIONS TO
> ACHIEVE PROJECTED RESULTS.

HOW THIS TOOL WORKS:

1. Take a long, overdo look at yourself and your people. Rate yourself on these items:

   a. Your typical way of interacting with them.

   b. Your willingness to give feedback and recognition to them.

   c. Your style of "passing on" information to them.

   d. Your ability to engage them in participative decision-making.

2. Admit to yourself and to your staff that "things could be better" in the above areas if you would use, on a consistent basis, proper tools to do your job.

3. Begin a Self Development Program. Tell your staff that you need to improve the quality of your inter-personal interactions with them.

4. Announce the plans for this program during a staff meeting. Ask them for their support of your Development Program.

5. Share your plans in this way.

   a. Select specific tools of your trade which will help you become a better manager.

   b. Select a different staff member each month to act as your "monitor." This person will have permission to critique your behavior as you practice a specific Tool for that month.

6. Make available the following list of Tools to your staff.

   a. **Name Calling** when greeting people, when being introduced to people, when asking questions of people, when delegating work assignments to people.

   b. **Legitimizing a member's presence or absence** at the start of a meeting, to keep meeting attendees informed.

   c. **Setting an end-time** to all meetings and appointments to allow people to schedule effectively and efficiently their day's work.

   d. **Using assertive expressions** to let others know your needs and your opinions.

   e. **Getting understanding** of the other person's viewpoint without thinking you have to also agree with that viewpoint.

   f. **Paraphrasing** another person's comments when you feel you've missed a part of the entire message, or you want to check the accuracy of what you did hear.

   g. **Delegating** with authority and tracking your delegation to insure that the job gets done correctly and on time.

h. **Crediting** persons when such recognition is due them. **Giving constructive, negative feedback** when such situations demand it.

People have a right to know how they are doing in their work and how other people see their actions.

i. **Asking open-ended questions** of people. Open-ended questions allow people to give their opinions openly and freely.

j. **Owning problems** when they are yours. **Owning decisions** when some of the decisions go "against your wishes." Most people do not appreciate "problem pushers" or "buck passers."

k. **Coping with different opinions** when you need to. **Controlling your feelings** when you choose to.

7. Proceed to master the other Tools mentioned in **TRADE SECRETS.** Also, use the *Reinforcement Cards* which refer to each Tool. These "reinforcers" will become mind joggers for you as you build positive morale among your people.

(See *Reinforcement Cards*, pages 179 to 195.)

SITUATIONS:
- Needing to develop better interpersonal relationships.
- Confronting conditions which foster conflict-producing behaviors.
- Suggesting specific Tools for use when correcting certain malfunctions in work productivity rates.
- Taking steps to develop a work group into a team.
- Assessing listening skills to determine the source of continued misunderstandings.
- Confronting an employee who "harbors" a negative attitude toward work and customers.

- Holding meetings which seem to "rob" people of their discretionary time. By selecting proper meeting tools, these attendees will begin to understand the need for such meetings and they will more actively participate in discussing agenda items with sufficient knowledge and responsibility.
- Wanting to build positive morale.

BENEFITS AND PAYOFFS:

1. Results in greater productivity.

2. Reduces and/or eliminates the need for grievances.

3. Equips you with tools for handling negative emotions in a productive manner.

4. Teaches you to deal with conflict in its earliest stage.

5. Allows you to practice using an "open-door policy" properly.

6. Permits you to acknowledge publicly your mistakes without losing "face" with your staff.

7. Permits you to recognize and compliment your staff without being criticized for flattery.

8. Builds your self-esteem while encouraging others to build positive attitudes.

EXAMPLES OF PEOPLE USING THIS TOOL:

SOCIAL SETTING: Hotel Management

The manager of a particular hotel decided to host a "Manager's House Party" for his employees. It was his way of building positive morale — saying "thank you" — and showing that he cared enough to invest his time and money in their having a good time. He sent a memo saying:

"I am willing to do any job you request of me. The job may not exceed two hours. One member needs to schedule my jobs. While I'm doing your job, you are free to use your time on the premise. My job performance must be evaluated by the person requesting the work."

It worked! Within two months, the staff planned "A Manager's Roast" to give their manager his performance appraisal.

(The positive results of this party were visible in the quality of service and the volume of work output from his staff.)

* * *

BUSINESS SETTING: Office Management

The president of the company decided to manage her day by "wandering around." She left her office and began to see and talk to people of all ranks. With some, she spent her time learning how they tracked their delegations. With others, she heard about meetings that seem to last "forever." She complimented those people who took their time to "show her the ropes" of what they were doing.

She returned to her office after spending a worthwhile day "in the field." She held her next staff meeting. She was ready to do "battle" with meetings which did not specify end-times.

She institutionalized the Tool, TIME CONTRACTING. Her meeting would take forty minutes, 9:00-9:40 a.m. She requested each supervisor to become familiar with this Tool. (See TIME CONTRACTING TOOL, page 149.)

She was building positive morale!

CAUTION:

DON'T give "lip service" to the idea of building positive morale once you determine it is a real need of your group.

Reason: Most people are quick to detect false commitment to a project or movement. They are not willing initially, to give their support or trust because they do not believe anything different will occur. You'll have to prove to your group that you intend to take action on this project. Then, you'll need to constantly demonstrate to them that your action is real and will be measured in terms of achieving intended results.

DO become a person of your word! If you say you want to build positive morale — then — do it! Use the specific Tools mentioned in this book.

TROUBLESHOOTING:

"I'm using this tool and it doesn't seem to work for me."

NATURE OF DIFFICULTY — Problem

"I have a boss who feels he is a builder of positive morale because he has an 'open-door policy.' This policy simply means that anyone is free to speak with him. However, there are many 'ifs' attached to his policy. So, most of us don't bother to use it. I'd like to give him this feedback, but I'd have to work through too many 'ifs.' What do you suggest?"

SUGGESTIONS:

A. Write your concerns in a letter. Tell your boss that you would be available for further clarification, or more detail, if he would like to take advantage of *your* "open-door policy." You may wish to mark your letter/envelope, *"Confidential."*

B. Call his secretary and ask for an appointment. Inform his secretary that the nature of your meeting will deal with interpretations of his "open-door policy."

C. Deal with the issue of confidentiality when you write to him or meet with him. This seems to be the main reason why most people do not choose to exercise their right to speak with him.

D. Realize that maintaining positive morale and an "open-door policy" are not necessarily the same! Both concepts are subject to interpretation by their authors and users. These interpretations must be understood by both groups. Otherwise, both concepts are "dead in the water."

NOTE: BELIEVE IT OR NOT, PEOPLE HAVE AN INSATIABLE NEED TO ENHANCE THEIR SELF-ESTEEM. THEY ALSO HAVE A DOMINANT NEED TO BE WINNERS. BY USING THESE TWO MOTIVATIONAL PRINCIPLES, YOU WILL BUILD POSITIVE MORALE AMONG YOUR PEOPLE. START BY GETTING YOUR PEOPLE TO BELIEVE THAT THEY ARE WINNERS! USE THIS TOOL AND YOU'LL BE WORKING WITH A **TRADE SECRET**.

TOOL 5

CONTROLLING PERSONAL FEELINGS

DEFINITION:

A TOOL WHICH HELPS YOU GET IN TOUCH WITH YOUR FEELINGS AND LEARN TO CONTROL OR REGAIN CONTROL OF THEM THROUGH A SCHEDULING PROCESS. CHOOSING TO CONTROL YOUR FEELINGS HELPS YOU MAINTAIN YOUR MENTAL HEALTH AND SELF-ESTEEM.

HOW THIS TOOL WORKS:

1. Focus your attention on your *present feeling*. Simply pause for about five seconds and ask yourself, *"How do I feel right now?"*

   Let's say you answer the question this way, *"I feel upset."* (Note the feeling word you have used.)

2. Determine the origin of this feeling. Did you consciously choose it or did someone choose it for you?

   ### Here's Some Advice

   You choose your own feelings when you hear yourself making comments like these:

   a. *"I am furious."*

   b. *"Why do I let myself get angry?"*

   c. *"If I keep a cool head when I hear remarks like that, I'll be better off."*

   Someone chooses your feelings for you when you hear yourself making comments like these:

   a. *"He makes me furious."*

   b. *"Why does she do this to me?"*

   c. *"If he hadn't made that remark, I wouldn't be so upset."*

3. If you choose your own feelings, consider doing the following:

   Continue feeling the way you do or decide to change the way you feel. With either decision, use self-talk.

   HERE'S HOW:

   a. Schedule-in talk for *continuing* with your present feeling.

      "I am going to stay upset because I want to."

   b. Schedule-out talk for *changing* your present feeling.

      "I no longer want to feel this way. I've had it! I'm putting my attention on other things."

4. If you have allowed someone else to choose the way you now feel, consider doing the following:

   Continue to allow someone else to choose your feelings or decide to *regain your power* to choose how you want to feel. With either decision use self-talk.

   HERE'S HOW:

   a. Schedule-in talk for *continuing to allow someone else* to choose your feelings.

      "She makes me so upset. The things she says would make anyone feel terrible! She wrecked my day."

   b. Schedule-out talk for *regaining* your power to choose how you want to feel.

      "It's stupid to let her make me upset. How could I have allowed her such power over me. I'll cope my own way. I don't have to stay upset. I'll feel the way I want to."

5. Choose to be or not to be in control of your feelings. You own them. When you choose to let others control you, you're *allowing them to share some of your personal power.* However, you're still "in control." And, if you want to regain your personal power, you can! It's up to you.

SITUATIONS:

- Conversing and becoming bothered by the tone and content of the speaker.
- Working with a procrastinator.
- Waiting in line and becoming impatient with a slow clerk.
- Feeling "out-of-control" in a situation.
- Receiving a compliment or a criticism.
- Experiencing a traumatic or happy event.
- Dealing constructively with guilt or worry. (Since both feelings tend to *immobilize* a person, choose to schedule-out such feelings and live in the now.)
- Handling compliments. (Many people do not feel okay when they receive compliments.) Learn to schedule-in good feelings. It's healthy for your self-esteem.

BENEFITS AND PAYOFFS:

1. Keeps you in control of your present and future feelings.

2. Sharpens your awareness in determining when someone else is choosing your feelings for you.

3. Nourishes your mental health. You begin to realize feelings are reactions that you choose to have or not to have.

4. Allows you to live as an "in-charge" person.

5. Forces you to realistically deal with personal and interpersonal problems without placing blame on others for the way you feel.

6. Allows you to confront immobilizing feelings such as guilt and worry. Guilt deals with the past and worry deals with the future. (See *Your Erroneous Zones* by Dr. Wayne Dyer.)

7. Makes you own your ability to be responsible for the way you feel.

8. Motivates you to choose feelings based on actual, possible payoffs you will receive from those feelings.

9. Helps you learn how to make situations work for you rather than against you.

10. Stops feeding your erroneous zones (self-defeating thoughts) which create negative feelings and low self-esteem.

11. Develops, within you, a growing appreciation for valuing present moments.

EXAMPLES OF PEOPLE USING THIS TOOL:

SOCIAL SETTING

"This cold has really taken its toll on me and it makes me feel awful."

(The cold virus has charge of the person's feelings.)

* * *

SOCIAL SETTING

"I'm not feeling very well now, but by tomorrow, I know I'll feel better."

(This person chooses his present feeling, then decides to schedule it out. Finally, he chooses another feeling and schedules it in.)

* * *

BUSINESS SETTING

"I like raising my voice at staff meetings. At least it gets my staff's attention and that's what counts."

(This person chooses to feel "tough." He enjoys the payoffs he gets when he feels this way.)

* * *

BUSINESS SETTING

"My supervisor wants me to record all miscellaneous expenses. She makes me mad — as if I were cheating her out of money . . ."

(This employee has given some of her power away to her supervisor. She is "not in charge" of her own feelings at this time.)

CAUTION:

DON'T fool yourself into thinking that controlling your feelings is an easy task to accomplish.

Reason: We are creatures of habit! We have conditioned ourselves to react a certain way in familiar situations. We have also developed a comfortable feeling about reacting the way we do, even if we choose good or bad feelings. We have the power to control our feelings, but we usually "put up a fight" when confronted with any change to our normal way of acting.

For a number of years we have reinforced these feelings so we can now choose them spontaneously. Then, one day we learn that we can change and control the way we feel. An easy task? Hardly! We need to *unlearn* what we have *learned* about feelings.

DO realize it takes approximately 21 days to change a behavior or habit. It also takes continual reinforcement. You need to develop new ways of thinking, rather than thinking what did happen or what will happen.

When you find yourself reacting with a feeling you no longer wish to have, schedule it out by positive self-talk. Schedule in a positive feeling — one that gives you more positive payoffs. With determination, you will succeed.

TROUBLESHOOTING:

"I'm using this tool and it doesn't seem to work for me."

NATURE OF DIFFICULTY — Problem

"A business associate of mine can never get to an appointment on time. Whenever I go with him, he always makes me late. I get upset and blame him for making me late. Now, according to the Steps in this Tool, I can choose not to get upset. Well, I tried it and it doesn't work! Believe me — I'd like it to work, but it doesn't. Any suggestions?"

SUGGESTIONS:

A. Use assertive talk. Tell the associate you will leave at a certain time. If he is not ready, you will see him at the meeting. Then, follow through on your commitment. (You are scheduling "in" an assertive feeling and you are staying in control.)

B. Ask the associate to specify a time for leaving. If it is not acceptable to you, negotiate. (See TIME CONTRACTING TOOL, Step #3, page 149.)

C. Decide, before traveling to the meeting, that you will not schedule "in" any upset feelings. Instead, schedule "in" positive feelings and visualize yourself with these feelings before beginning your travel plans.

D. Review each Step of this Tool and know that it takes 21 days to condition yourself out of a habit that you no longer want to practice. In the meantime, start visualizing and reinforcing new habits of thinking and feeling.

NOTE: DR. WAYNE DYER, AUTHOR OF *YOUR ERRONEOUS ZONES*, BELIEVES THAT YOU ARE THE SUM TOTAL OF ALL YOUR CHOICES. YOU HAVE THE POWER TO CHOOSE YOUR FEELINGS — YOUR THOUGHTS — YOUR ACTIONS. SO, CHOOSE FEELINGS THAT REFLECT WHO YOU ARE. THEN, LET YOUR ACTIONS REFLECT THOSE FEELINGS. USE THIS TOOL AND YOU WILL BE USING A **TRADE SECRET**.

TOOL 6

COPING WITH DIFFERENT OPINIONS

DEFINITION:

A TOOL FOR UNDERSTANDING ANOTHER PERSON'S OPINION WITHOUT NECESSARILY HAVING TO FEEL THE SAME WAY ABOUT IT AS THE PERSON DOES. USERS OF THIS TOOL CAN RECOGNIZE, ACCEPT AND UNDERSTAND A DIFFERENT VIEWPOINT WITHOUT HAVING TO CHANGE IT, SHARE IT, ADOPT IT, OR EVEN APPROVE IT.

HOW THIS TOOL WORKS:

1. Give your *full attention* to the speaker. (Your *entire body* is *facing* the speaker; your *eyes* are *focused* on theirs; your *mind* is *open* to the speaker's idea — you are not thinking about anything else.)

2. Listen to the idea and recognize that the speaker holds a different opinion on the subject than you do.

3. Tell the speaker that you have a different opinion.

   "Mr. Whittier, I have a different opinion on the subject."

   Option: You may not want to tell the speaker in certain situations. However, tell yourself that you "see it" differently.

4. Keep your mind open to what the speaker is saying. This is a difficult process!

5. Accept the fact that it's all right for this person to have a different viewpoint than yours.

6. Tell the speaker that his opinion is acceptable to you.

   "Mr. Whittier, I accept the fact that we hold different opinions and it's okay."

7. Continue to work at understanding the different viewpoint by actively listening to what the speaker is saying.

   "I'm understanding your viewpoint much better now. You're really angry with the way customers take advantage of our refund policy. Please continue, Mr. Whittier."

   (If necessary, refer to the ACTIVE LISTENING TOOL, page 1.)

8. Use nonverbals and/or verbal expressions to inform the speaker that you empathize with his thoughts.

   (An *affirmative nod of your head* or a *focused eye* will convey your feelings of empathy.)

SITUATIONS:
- Talking with people who think differently than you.
- Engaging in heated arguments when it becomes obvious that neither party is listening. If you are one of the parties, use this Tool. If you are a third party, use this Tool in a facilitative manner.
- Counseling a client.
- Discussing the advantages and disadvantages of a product.
- Talking with aggressive-type personalities.
- Appraising employees' performances.
- Negotiating terms of a contract, agreement, etc.
- Selling an item to a potential customer.
- Overcoming verbal resistance from another person.
- Giving a reprimand or negative feedback to someone.
- Wanting to show an attitude of care and concern toward a person who worries.
- Settling formal and informal disputes.

BENEFITS AND PAYOFFS:

1. Enables you and others to achieve mutual understanding between persons.

2. Places you within the other person's frame of reference and allows you to look at the issue through his or her eyes.

3. Allows other persons the *freedom* to express their ideas without you "correcting their thinking" when it differs from yours.

4. Gives you freedom to listen open-mindedly to the other's opinion. As a result, you feel comfortable in recognizing, accepting and understanding the opinion and you express this feeling to the person.

5. Enhances the other person's self-esteem by your showing the person you care to listen to what he or she thinks.

6. Allows you to maintain a non-evaluative listening posture.

   (This posture is the most effective agent we know for helping another person improve his or her relationships and communications with others.)

7. Demonstrates a caring attitude on your part toward another person's values, beliefs and opinions.

8. Communicates the idea that you want to understand the other's point of view and the feelings that come with that point of view, without feeling exactly like the other person.

9. Permits people to "drop" their defenses and speak honestly to you.

10. Encourages you to do effective problem solving on a rational-emotive base, rather than problem solving only on a rational base.

EXAMPLES OF PEOPLE USING THIS TOOL:

SOCIAL SETTING

(Two neighbors, Larry and Tom, are disputing the placement of a fence.)

Tom: *"We're arguing because we see things differently. I know my views, but I don't really understand yours. I need your help, Larry. I want to understand your views on this matter. Go slowly so I'll get everything you are saying."*

(This approach may lead to a compromise and improved communications. Remember, Tom does not have to *buy in* to the opinion of Larry.)

* * *

FAMILY SETTING

(A mother and her college-age daughter are having a discussion.)

Daughter: *"I don't have time, in the morning, to straighten my bedroom. I don't understand why it bothers you. After all, I close my door so you don't have to look at it."*

Mother: *"I recognize that we have different opinions on this subject, Mary. I understand your reason for closing your door and your frustration with me for not accepting your solution to the situation. Let's see if we can find a workable compromise that will satisfy both of us."*

* * *

BUSINESS SETTING

(A doctor is talking with his patient.)

Doctor: *"Max, I want to better understand your point of view. Give me some background on why you feel the medicine is causing you more trouble than it's worth."*

* * *

BUSINESS SETTING

(A project manager wants to understand the reason why his team member took a different approach on one phase of their project.)

Manager: *"Roger, what led you to develop the second phase of the project this way. I don't understand and I want to."*

* * *

BUSINESS SETTING

(A director and her department head hold different opinions regarding budget expenditures.)

Director: *"Jackie, we don't think alike. We don't have to! But we do need to understand each other's thinking. So, I need you to explain to me again, what your key points are regarding our cost expenditures."*

CAUTION:

DON'T *pretend* to empathize with a person who holds opinions you cannot understand, or do not wish to understand.

Reason: Most people are quick to see that you are being manipulative, condescending or dishonest with them. Polite mannerisms (pretending to be empathetic) are often a conscious or subconscious disguise for dishonest feelings.

DO make a conscious effort to empathize with another person whose views are different from yours. Pretense and disguised politeness are not attributes of empathy.

TROUBLESHOOTING:

"I'm using this tool and it doesn't seem to work for me."

NATURE OF DIFFICULTY — Problem

"I have a customer who is frequently late with her loan payment. She usually explains her reasons for being late. I find myself sympathizing with her and I know I should be practicing empathy rather than sympathy. Help me out."

SUGGESTIONS:

A. Clear up your confusion with sympathy and empathy. Realize that sympathy is the process of feeling the *same way* another person feels. Empathy is the process of understanding the other's opinion and the way the other feels about it *without having to feel the same way yourself.*

B. Review the Steps of this Tool under the heading, HOW THIS TOOL WORKS, page 37.

C. Realize that in your situation, there are more *negative payoffs* for sympathizing with your customer than you need.

   Here are two negative payoffs:

   — Physical fatigue from carrying the same intense feeling as she does.

   — Anxiety from allowing her lateness to "get to you" which results in her continued late behavior and your not receiving her loan payment on time.

NATURE OF DIFFICULTY — Problem

"I had a conversation the other night with my son. I'm trying to steer him in the direction of taking computer science courses in senior high. He keeps telling me that he is not interested in this field. In fact, last night, he said that I wasn't trying to understand his point of view. Wow — and I'm supposed to be doing a better job of coping with different opinions! Any suggestions?"

SUGGESTIONS:

A. Go back and review Step #1 in the Section, HOW THIS TOOL WORKS, page 37. Follow this Step exactly.

B. Go on to the next Step and then begin to visualize, in your mind, the conversation. (See VISUALIZING TOOL, page 171.)

C. Tell your son that you want to understand his point of view and keep an open mind to what he tells you. When you understand what he is saying, say so.

D. Assess the situation at this point. If you want to share your opinion, and I know you do, then, ask your son if he would like to hear your views.

> Parent: *"I can understand your views much better now, Mark. Would you be interested in my perspective?"*
>
> (If he says, *"No,"* then do not pursue the matter at this time because you do not have a listener!)

NOTE: YOUR KEY TO SUCCESS, WHEN DEALING WITH PEOPLE WHO HAVE DIFFERENT OPINIONS FROM YOURS, IS TO RESPOND WITH EMPATHY. ALSO, USE THIS TOOL WHEN HANDLING CUSTOMER COMPLAINTS. "ZERO IN" ON THE CONTENT AND THE FEELING OF THE COM-PLAINER AND RESPOND WITH EMPATHY. IT WORKS! IT'S A **TRADE SECRET!**

TOOL 7
CREDITING

DEFINITION:

A TOOL FOR RECOGNIZING THE WORK EFFORTS OF A PERSON OR GROUP. IT'S "GIVING CREDIT WHERE CREDIT IS DUE" AND REMEMBERING TO DO IT!

HOW THIS TOOL WORKS:

1. Know what's going on with your people and whose contributions and ideas deserve special notice. Do not skip this step!

   PROCESS:

   a. Walk around and observe. This is "first-hand evidence."

   b. Read up-dates of people's work as "second-hand evidence."

   c. Listen to what others tell you about certain individuals and verify the data.

2. Let the deserving person know you appreciate what he or she is doing or has done. Address the person by name either verbally or in writing.

   VERBAL FORM:

   "Tony, I want to commend you for your quick reply to that customer's request. I appreciate your concern."

   WRITTEN FORM:

   "Fine job, Bill. I told the boss the entire package was yours. We're looking good!"

3. Let others know "who did what" when such circumstances occur. Give either verbal or written credit. At times, you may want to give credit in both forms.

   VERBAL CREDIT:

   "Sue deserves credit for recommending this action, Joe." (Then, at a later time, let Sue know you gave her credit at its proper time.)

   WRITTEN CREDIT:

   "Your memo says, 'Due to Charlie's efforts, we have reached our quota for October. We did it in only two weeks. Congratulations!'"

4. Be genuine by speaking or writing honestly.

   It is a trade secret to know that "honesty is your best policy and flattery will get you nowhere."

5. Be sure to give someone in your family or on the job some credit or a compliment *every day*.

6. **Option Step:** On a weekly basis, evaluate your "credit rating." Use these questions:

   a. *"How is my credit rating with my office staff?"*

   b. *"How often do I express my appreciation to certain members in my family?"*

   Develop a monitoring sheet for reinforcement purposes. Keep this sheet private!

   HERE'S HOW:

   — Place peoples' names along left side of sheet.
   — Place days of month at top of sheet.
   — Put a check next to each person's name when you have given that person some type of credit.
   — Begin to notice a pattern in your credit behavior.

Name	Day	1	2	3	4	5	6	7	8	9	10	11	12	13	14	15	16	17	18	19	20	21	22	23	24	25	26	27	28	29	30	31
1.																																
2.																																
3.																																
4.																																
5.																																
6.																																

Month:

SITUATIONS:

- Conducting or participating in staff meetings.
- Getting others to work together effectively in group settings by mentioning (periodically) their unique contributions.
- Introducing new people and citing their talents.
- Recognizing the efforts of certain family members to build family spirit.
- Appraising someone's work performance.
- Receiving compliments for your work unit and remembering to "pass them on" to their owners.
- Announcing awards for project completions.
- Giving constructive feedback.
- Writing correspondence which specifies the work efforts of certain individuals or departments.
- Saying "Thank you" and making eye contact with the person. (These two actions need to be done simultaneously.)

BENEFITS AND PAYOFFS:

1. Shares positional power with deserving staff members.

2. Honors the talents, skills and expertise of an individual or group.

3. Builds positive morale, especially in group settings. (This only occurs when the *credit given* is perceived by the group members as *credit due!*)

4. Eliminates the "Lip-Service-Syndrome" from people who say they believe in "giving credit where it's due" but *never* find the time to give it.

5. Adds to an individual's reputation by publicly recognizing his or her role and function on a specific work effort.

6. Bestows honor and esteem on supervisors and their staffs by focusing attention on certain specialized skills of their staff members.

7. Provides opportunities for employers and others to practice honesty and fairness when dealing with the work performance of people.

8. Shows positive regard toward others by making them feel valued and needed — and people need to be needed!

9. Provides a person with an occasion to give genuine feedback while helping him or her develop self-confidence in giving this feedback.

EXAMPLES OF PEOPLE USING THIS TOOL:

SOCIAL SETTING: Restaurant

(Two people are enjoying their dinners and raving about the tastiness of their dishes. A waiter approaches their table and says:)

Waiter: *"Well, is everything all right here?"*

Patron: *"Yes, these seafood dishes are delicious. We were just raving about them."*

Waiter: *"Fine, I'm glad you like them. I'll tell the chef how much you enjoy his cooking."*

* * *

FAMILY SETTING: Discussion

(It's Saturday morning and the house needs cleaning. The dining room table and kitchen table are cluttered with school work and dated newspapers. Tom, a ten year old, decides to help his mother by cleaning the tables. Later that day, his mother compliments him for the fine job he did without his being asked to do it. She says:)

"Tom, I'm really glad you helped me this morning. It's great to come home to a clean house. Thanks. You made my day!"

* * *

BUSINESS SETTING

(A manager is giving credit to his supervisor.)

Manager: *"Bill, thank you for suggesting the idea of placing an end-time on our meetings. Your idea is working and we are benefitting from it."*

* * *

BUSINESS SETTING

(Harry is discussing his department's budget format with Ralph, his boss.)

Harry: *"It was Marcia's idea to structure the format this way. I am not going to take credit for it. I'll let her know that you think her idea is an excellent one, Ralph."*

* * *

BUSINESS SETTING: Written Correspondence

"Captain Smith's reorganization of the Comptroller's Office is proceeding on schedule."

CAUTION:

DON'T take credit for an idea, suggestion or solution that does not rightfully belong to you.

Reason: Most people can easily detect when you are taking something that does not belong to you. It's called "shoplifting" in stores and "stealing" in other places. Besides, most people who deserve the credit will discover that you usually "take all the credit" when it's really their work effort that makes you look so good!

DO acknowledge the fact that your people deserve full credit for work efforts they accomplish. Be quick to recognize this fact. Give your people credit every day, if necessary. It won't hurt them and it won't hurt you. Credit can only hurt when it is expected and not given, or when you don't mean what you say.

TROUBLESHOOTING:

"I'm using this tool and it doesn't seem to work for me."

NATURE OF DIFFICULTY — Problem

"During one of our staff meetings, we were tasked to develop a list of advantages/disadvantages for using flex time in our organization. We were supposed to ask our work units for their ideas. When we returned the following week, a department head shared her ideas as if all the ideas were hers. She kept using the expression, 'I think . . .' Now, I know her group gave her many ideas. Obviously, she took all the credit! I want to give her some feedback. What do I say to her?"

SUGGESTIONS:

A. Ask the department head some clarifying questions.
   - *"Who surfaced those kinds of ideas, Marge?"*
   - *"What did you have in mind when you thought of that idea, Marge?"*
   - *"What were some of the ideas of your staff, Marge?"*

B. Suggest that when people make reports of this kind, they use the pronoun "We," or the phrase, "Some of my staff members," or the names of the contributors.

* * *

NATURE OF DIFFICULTY — Problem

"Sometimes I forget to credit some of my technicians for resolving computer programming problems. I seem to recall the oversight 'after the fact.' What do you recommend?"

SUGGESTIONS:

A. Find a suitable time and speak honestly to the individual. Most of the time, such individuals are pleased to know that you know "who's" doing "what." Remember, it's never too late to congratulate!

B. Make a self-disclosure statement in private, or, if possible, in front of the group.

   "Jan, I failed to acknowledge your effort in resolving our major computer problem. It was an oversight on my part and I apologize. I commend you for pursuing the problem to its resolution. Thank you and any other person who helped in this effort."

NOTE: PEOPLE TEND TO SUPPORT WHAT THEY HELP CREATE. IF WHAT THEY CREATE IS WORTHY OF RECOGNITION AND PRAISE, GIVE IT! THEN, YOU WILL UNDERSTAND WHY CREDITING IS A **TRADE SECRET**.

TOOL 8
DECISION OWNERSHIP

DEFINITION:

A TOOL FOR HELPING PEOPLE DEAL WITH DECISIONS IN WHICH THEY HAVE OR HAVE NOT BEEN PART OF THE DECISION-MAKING PROCESS. USERS OF THIS TOOL NEED TO OWN, SUPPORT AND IMPLEMENT ACTION-ORIENTED PROCEDURES FOR EACH DECISION.

HOW THIS TOOL WORKS:

1. Listen with *your full attention* to the person giving you the decision. Or, read all written decisions thoroughly.

2. Develop an understanding of the decision in terms of its source, its rationale, its parameters and its responsibilities.

   HERE'S HOW:

   a. Ask clarifying questions when necessary.
      - If the decision is contrary to your beliefs, values or way of operating, work to change the decision when possible.
      - If you are unable to change the decision, *work to develop an adequate understanding of it and support it.* You are not free to ignore the decision or to sabotage it in any way!

   b. Restate the decision for an accuracy check.

   c. **Remember:** In the process of understanding a decision, you do not need to agree or disagree with the decision. (See UNDERSTANDING AGREEMENT OR DISAGREEMENT TOOL, page 157.)

3. Own and support the decision to the best of your ability. *Liking or disliking the decision is not essential to your owning it.*

4. Use verbal or written expressions to communicate your ownership of the decision, regardless of your involvement in the decision-making process.

Here are some expressions to use:

"I need you to . . ."

"My top priority at this moment is . . ."

"We need your expertise on . . ."

Here are some expressions not to use:

"He told me we had to do it."

"They just said, 'Do it.'"

"She wants . . ."

5. Use action-oriented procedures and implement the decision. Take ultimate responsibility for its completion within the scope of your authority.

Action-oriented procedures:

   a. Identify what is to be done.

   b. Describe its parameters.

   c. Assign proper resources.

   d. Monitor progress to its completion.

SITUATIONS:

- Attending a meeting where decisions have been made and you are informed about them.
- Receiving a memo indicating a decision has been made affecting your department.

- Hearing an announcement of a decision that is contrary to your liking and your way of operating.
- Having to attend meetings which are imposed on you.
- Communicating a decision to your staff.
- Supporting an action dictated by upper management.
- Writing a delegation to one of your employees. The delegation involves a previously made decision.

BENEFITS AND PAYOFFS:

1. Places power for decision implementation in your hands. Realigns power bases in your favor.

2. Builds your commitment to organizational policies and procedures. What you do not know — you now find out! You tend to ask more questions because you have a "right to know."

3. Improves your delegations. They are more complete!

4. Insures mutual understanding of rationale for decisions delegated to you and decisions you delegate to others.

5. Encourages rapport between and among your co-workers or supervisors, because each person owns a share in the decision and its implementation.

6. Demonstrates your support for various roles, functions and goals of your organization or company.

7. Boosts organizational morale when your people know that you understand, support and intend to implement decisions.

8. Builds a sense of teamwork by owning simple and difficult decisions made by you or others.

9. Strengthens the chain-of-command because you use the "chain" to its best advantage. There are no "weak links!"

10. Helps you apply your expertise when dealing with decisions you don't like.

EXAMPLES OF PEOPLE USING THIS TOOL:

SOCIAL SETTING

(It's Saturday. The family has just finished eating breakfast. George, their 10 year old son, and his mother are still at the table.)

Mother: *"Your father wants you to clean your room, George."*

George: *"Why do you say it like that, Mom? Don't you want me to do it, too?"*

Mother: *"Yes, of course I do."*

George: *"Then why say Dad? As if you don't want to have to tell me to do something. Why don't you just tell it like it is, Mom?"*

(He is asking his mother to own the decision.)

Mother: *"What are you telling me, George?"*

George: *"Mom, if you and Dad want me to do something, then say, 'We want you to do . . .' If it's just you wanting me to do something, then tell me just that way. I'm asking you to just say what you really mean!"*

(His mother is learning how to own decisions.)

Mother: *"Okay, George. We want you to clean your room this morning."*

(She owns the decision along with her husband.)

George: *"I get the message."*

* * *

BUSINESS SETTING

(After attending a directors' meeting, Joel sets up a staff meeting to inform his people of some decisions affecting their work units. His meeting is in session.)

Joel: *"I am concerned about our use of overtime during the last quarter. In fact, all of the departments are looking into this matter. We have decided to review the need . . ."*

(Joel received the decision at his earlier meeting and is owning the decision as a member of management. Note the approach he takes with his people.)

CAUTION:

DON'T, on a frequent basis, use other peoples' names to pass on difficult decisions.

Reason: Many times, people think you are "passing the buck" when you quote someone else's name on decisions that you find difficult to support. Often, using a name other than your own, reduces your position to a power-less position or a position devoid of authority. Owning a decision demonstrates responsible, accountable, authoritative power. You need to exercise this power. Use it to your advantage!

DO use your own name or the personal pronoun "I" which communicates to others your ownership of the decision. Your position requires this degree of responsibility from you.

TROUBLESHOOTING:

"I'm using this tool and it doesn't seem to work for me."

NATURE OF DIFFICULTY — Problem

"A few of my employees are abusing the flex-time pro-cedures. They continue to arrive several minutes late each morning! These same employees tend to leave early at the end of the day. They're not working a full eight-hour day. To remedy the situation, upper manage-ment made a decision to use Sign-In and Sign-Out Sheets.

Now, I don't like this decision and I'm finding it very difficult to tell my staff to follow it. I need help!"

SUGGESTIONS:

A. Ask more questions of upper management to deepen your understanding of the decision. You need to achieve adequate understanding even to own it. Remember, you do not need to agree with it, but you must understand it, support it and implement it to the best of your ability. *You do not need to tell your staff that you disagree with it.*

B. Use the following statement when communicating the decision to your staff:

"I need each of you to begin signing in when you arrive at work and to sign out when you leave work at the end of your day. The reason for this new policy is . . ."

C. Be careful to avoid "blaming statements." Although you are not a member of upper management, you still are considered management. Support the team! Don't "pass the buck!"

NOTE: DECISION OWNERSHIP GIVES YOU FREEDOM TO ACT. "PASSING THE BUCK" GIVES YOU FREEDOM TO REACT! CHOOSE WHICH TYPE OF FREEDOM YOU WANT. REMEMBER, OWNING A DECISION THAT YOU ARE SUPPOSED TO OWN IS A **TRADE SECRET**.

TOOL 9

DEFOGGING

DEFINITION:

A TOOL FOR GETTING ACCOUNTABLE, PRECISE ANSWERS FROM ALL TYPES OF "FOGGERS." IN ORDER TO USE THIS TOOL PROPERLY, KNOWLEDGE ABOUT FOGGING IS ESSENTIAL. IF NECESSARY, SEE TOOL 12 ON **FOGGING,** PAGE

HOW THIS TOOL WORKS:

1. Listen and be able to recognize a fogging response to your question or remark.

An Example

You: *"What's the status on the Crane account, Mike?"*

Mike: *"We're working on it."*
(Fogging)

* * *

An Example

You: *"You look tired today, Sue."*

Sue: *"Perhaps I do."*
(Fogging)

2. Defog either type of response by asking a clarifying question.

An Example

You: *"What's the status on the Crane account, Mike?"*

Mike: *"We're working on it."*
(Fogging)

You: *"What does that mean, Mike?"*
(Clarifying question)

* * *

An Example

You: *"You look tired today, Sue."*

Sue: *"Perhaps I do."*
(Fogging)

You: *"What might be causing you to look tired, Sue?"*
(Clarifying question)

3. Wait for the person's reply.

   a. If you are satisfied with the answer, then stop. You have successfully defogged the conversation to your satisfaction.

   b. If you are not satisfied with the answer, continue to ask clarifying questions until you feel satisfied.

   SOME CLARIFYING QUESTIONS:

   — *"What specific work has been done to date, Mike?"*

   — *"When will you complete these last two items, Mike?"*

   — *"What time today, Mike?"*

4. **Option Step:** Use a self-disclosure statement when you do not understand fogging responses.

A Self-Disclosure Statement:

"I don't understand your last comment. I need more clarity on the status of the Crane account. Help me out, Mike. Who is working on the account and when will it arrive on my desk?"
(Clarifying questions)

5. Know that when you ask specific questions to clarify a situation, you are defogging!

SITUATIONS:

- Seeking accountability in verbal and written communications.
- Dealing effectively with habitual "foggers."
- Acquiring precise data for briefing meetings.
- Confronting a person whose daily work performance is unsatisfactory.
- Needing to get "the real story" on an area of concern.
- Setting priorities on a back-log of work.
- Getting answers that make sense to you.

BENEFITS AND PAYOFFS:

1. Keeps work production on schedule and lets you know when and why it's behind schedule.

2. Helps you to avoid misunderstandings which occur when you receive general, noncommittal-type answers.

3. Eliminates your need to make assumptions.

4. Keeps your people accountable and responsible.

5. Gives you an opportunity to dispel and eventually destroy "rumor mills."

6. Allows you to give constructive feedback to "foggers."

7. Keeps you informed and up-to-date.

8. Saves you time and money. You learn to ask the right questions at the right time.

EXAMPLES OF PEOPLE USING THIS TOOL:

— *"What does that mean?"*

— *"I don't understand that comment. Will you please clarify it for me?"*

— *"Who will be getting in touch with me?"*

— *"How do you want this report done?"*

— *"I will get back in touch with you on Thursday. When, on Thursday, would be a good time to call you?"*

* * *

BUSINESS SETTING

(Due to a malfunction in her computer terminal, Sara calls the Computer Center to check on the status of her unit.)

Sara:	*"I'm calling to check on the status of my unit. My service repair number is S-0784."*
Office Clerk:	*"They're working on it."* (Fogging)
Sara:	*"What does that mean?"* (Defogging)
Office Clerk:	*"I don't know. You'll have to talk to Service. Shall I connect you?"*
Sara:	*"Yes."*
Service:	*"What is your repair number please?"*
Sara:	*"Repair number S-0784. What is its status?"* (Defogging)

Service: *"It's on the workbench now. I'll call you in one hour and let you know when you can pick it up."*
(Precise answer)

Sara: *"Fine. If I don't hear from you in one hour, I'll call you back. Thank you."*
(Self-disclosure statement)

CAUTION:

DON'T use sarcastic tones or aggressive behaviors on "foggers." There are better ways to get precise, accountable answers from these people.

Reason: Some people are not aware of their fogging habits. There are other people who are aware and deliberately intend to "put you off" with fogging responses. In both instances, if you were to use sarcasm or aggressive tactics, you would offend their right to be spoken to respectfully.

DO use defogging tactics such as: clarifying questions, self-disclosure statements and other assertive expressions to acquire adequate understanding of "foggy" situations.

TROUBLESHOOTING:

"I'm using this tool and it doesn't seem to work for me."

NATURE OF DIFFICULTY — Problem

"One of my employees has been doing unsatisfactory work for the past week. When I asked him how things were going, he said, 'Fine.' When I asked him what that meant, he said, 'things are moving along.' Now, I think he's a first-class fogger. I need help. What's my next move?"

SUGGESTIONS:

A. Continue to defog his remarks. You may need to ask more precise questions.

HERE IS AN EXAMPLE:

"What three items have you been working on since Tuesday, Fred?"

(Sometimes, people make unintentional fog responses. This situation occurs when these people are asked poorly worded questions! Such questions lack specificity.) Note: The example question above is very specific.

B. If necessary, use self-disclosure statements to let him know that you are having trouble understanding what he actually means.

HERE IS AN EXAMPLE:

"Fred, I'm having trouble understanding your comments. I need you to be more specific with me. For example . . ."

(For references, see the TOOL on OPEN-ENDED QUESTIONS, page 9, and the TOOL on BEING ASSERTIVE, page 15.)

NOTE: THIS TOOL NEEDS EXPERT HANDLING. RE-MEMBER, ASKING WELL-WORDED QUESTIONS, MAKING SELF-DISCLOSURE STATEMENTS AND USING RESPECTFUL TONES WILL HELP YOU TO GAIN MASTERY OF THIS TOOL IN A SHORT PERIOD OF TIME. YOU WILL NEED TO USE THIS TOOL DAILY BECAUSE THE WORLD IS FULL OF FOGGERS. SO, KNOWING HOW TO DEFOG IS A **TRADE SECRET.**

TOOL 10

DELEGATING

DEFINITION:

A TOOL FOR GETTING QUALITY WORK DONE BY TAPPING THE RESOURCES OF OTHER PEOPLE. USERS OF THIS TOOL ARE RESULTS-ORIENTED PEOPLE! THEY GIVE PROPER AUTHORITY, ESTABLISH FEEDBACK OR TRACKING SYSTEMS AND ASSIGN MUTUAL ACCOUNTABILITY FOR THEIR DELEGATIONS.

HOW THIS TOOL WORKS:

1. Be aware of two organizational prerequisites governing your ability to delegate effectively.

   a. The organization knows its priorities and the results it must accomplish to achieve those priorities.

   b. The organization holds its managers and supervisors accountable for achieving those results.

2. Identify the task/job that you need to delegate.

3. Select a capable and resourceful person (delegatee).

4. Explain the task to the delegatee in terms of its purpose, its priority and the specific results you need to achieve. Allow questions to surface.

   (The delegatee may need training to do this task and/or future tasks. Be willing to provide this requirement!)

5. Give sufficient authority to allow the delegatee to do the work. (Refer to the *Delegation-Action-Authority Form*, page 71.)

HERE'S HOW:

   a. Study the choices and select the most suitable one for your delegation.

   b. Attach the *Form* to your delegation and keep a carbon for your file.

6. Establish a feedback system for monitoring the progress and the completion of the work.

HERE ARE SOME METHODS:

   a. Schedule a progress/status date for the task at the same time that you give the delegatee the completion date. You are setting a mutually agreed-upon date for reporting purposes.

   b. Use a "Tickler System" to keep yourself updated on the number of delegations made to the same person or other persons. An accordian-type file with numbers (1-31) is appropriate. Slip the carbon *Delegation-Action-Authority Form* in its respective slot. Each day check the "tics" for that specific day.

7. Ask the delegatee to restate your delegation to insure mutual communication accuracy. (See PARA-PHRASING TOOL — Section: HOW THIS TOOL WORKS, Step #8, page 128.)

8. Document agreed upon terms.

SITUATIONS:

- Developing subordinates in delegation procedures.
- Utilizing other people's resources to their maximum.
- Empowering local managers with authority and accountability when distance becomes a vital factor in work accomplishment.
- Committing yourself to reducing your *In-Basket* load by delegating some of the work to capable people.
- Demonstrating trust and confidence in others.
- Resisting the urge to critique every piece of work in your office.

- Eliminating *time wasters* (doing tasks you should have delegated).
- Planning a vacation and needing someone to coordinate your activities while you are gone.
- Giving back a reverse delegation.
  (A reverse delegation occurs when a delegatee *gives back to you what you originally assigned the delegatee to do.* For instance, the delegatee says to you, *"Do you have time to work with me on this? Two heads are better than one."*)
  If you accept the offer, you become a victim of *reverse delegation.*

BENEFITS AND PAYOFFS:

1. Enables you to achieve effective delegations resulting in accomplishment of your goals.

2. Teaches you to stop wasting your time, efforts and money on delegating tasks based on misguided priorities and improper use of your peoples' time.

3. Equips you with a procedure for delegating with confidence — knowing that you have included the proper authority, specified the expected results, and used a tracking system to insure accountability.

4. Shows you how to establish a tickler system for insuring mutual accountability.

5. Provides opportunities for your employees to clarify problems "front-end" instead of tackling problems at their "back-end."

6. Helps you deal with priority conflicts by basing each delegation on an established set of priorities.

7. Saves you time, if you do it right!

8. Motivates your people to take responsibility and become accountable for what they do.

EXAMPLES OF PEOPLE USING THIS TOOL:

BUSINESS SETTING

This delegation involves Steps 1-8. Time: 12 minutes.

"John, I need you to conduct research on our 'comp-time' policy and procedures. A rough draft report would be fine." (The delegator identifies the task and selects the person.)

The delegator continues.

"Recently, several employees used this time and their supervisors questioned them about it. I know there are several interpretations on this policy. The morale is slipping because of people interpreting the policy any old way. I'm concerned. This task needs your immediate attention." (The delegator states the purpose of the task and its priority status.)

The delegator continues.

"You've got the authority to research this task, John. Give me some alternative actions with pros and cons for each. Then, I'd like you to recommend one for my approval." (The delegator gives the proper authority with the task.)

The delegator continues.

"I would like to get a progress report from you in three days and the final report in five days. How does this time frame fit your schedule?" (The delegator sets up a feedback system with the delegatee. Both discuss the suggested time frames. They agree on mutually acceptable dates.)

The delegator continues.

"John, what questions have you on this project?" (The delegator gives an opening for comments, questions.)

After the delegatee asks his questions, the delegator asks for a restatement of the delegation. The delegator makes a note of the transaction, gives the original to the delegatee, and places a copy in his tickler file under the proper "tic" date.

CAUTION:

DON'T *dump* or *unload* your undesirable work on others.

Reason: Many subordinates resent these "so-called" delegations as they feel their time and talents are not being used to their best advantage. They sense you just want to get rid of some work and with little or no explanation, you quickly tell them to "look this over" or "complete this when you have time."

DO take sufficient time to delegate each task. Include these elements in each delegation: purpose, priority status and completion date. Then, you'll never be accused of *dumping* or *unloading* on your subordinates.

TROUBLESHOOTING:

"I'm using this tool and it doesn't seem to work for me."

NATURE OF DIFFICULTY — Problem

"My tracking system isn't working. I'm using an accordian-type file with numbers corresponding to the days of the month. On any given day, I walk into the office, go to my file and retrieve the 'tics' for that day. I find myself spending most of the morning going after projects that are past due. How can I help my people become proactive and get their projects to me on or before their due date?"

SUGGESTIONS:

A. Be open with your employees and tell them you would appreciate receiving their projects on or before their "tic" dates. Be ready to handle many questions. You see, you have set up an agreed-upon date with them and, in some instances, you are asking them to report to you before that date.

Your tracking system is working! Your delegatees have due dates! However, instead of you tracking down your delegatees, ask them to make an appointment with you on the morning of their "tic" day. Tell them that they must initiate this meeting.

B. Ask them for suggestions regarding your problem. They may have a better solution than what is offered here.

C. Ask them what type of monitoring/tracking system they use to keep themselves accountable. Their answers may surprise you! They may not have any specific system in place. Their answers may give you valuable insights into the solution of your problem.

NOTE: TO MANAGE, YOU MUST DELEGATE. OTHER-WISE, YOU ARE NOT DOING YOUR JOB PROPERLY! TO DELEGATE, YOU MUST PLACE YOUR TRUST IN YOUR SUBORDINATES. THEIR ABILITIES WILL NEVER BE CHALLENGED UNLESS YOU DELEGATE WORK TO THEM. THIS IS A **TRADE SECRET!**

DELEGATION-ACTION-AUTHORITY
FORM

To: _____

From: _____

Date: _____

Re: _____

1. ☐ Take action — contact me if you feel it is necessary.

2. ☐ Take action — let me know what you did.

3. ☐ Look into this situation — let me know what you plan to do. Delay action until I give approval.

4. ☐ Look into this situation — give me possible alternative actions, with pros and cons. Please recommend one for approval.

5. ☐ Look into this situation — give me all the facts. I need to make the decision.

Remarks: _____

_____

_____

_____

TOOL 11

EYE POWER

DEFINITION:

A TOOL WHICH TAPS THE POWER RESOURCE OF THE EYE TO IMPROVE A PERSON'S LISTENING ABILITY. USERS OF THIS TOOL LEARN TO LISTEN WITH THEIR EYES, FOCUS THEIR EYES, WATCH FOR VISUAL CLUES AND RESPOND TO THE TOTAL MESSAGE OF THEIR SPEAKERS AND LISTENERS.

HOW THIS TOOL WORKS:

1. Become aware of the speaker's message by focusing your eyes on his or her eyes while you continue to listen with your ears.

2. Avoid staring.

3. Look away every 5-8 seconds by blinking or deflecting your eyes away from the speaker's eyes.

4. Learn to listen with your eyes! As you do this, you'll begin to notice certain "eye" behaviors.

   YOUR EYE BEHAVIORS:

   a. You tend to focus on one eye rather than on both eyes of the speaker when you're listening. Train yourself to focus and read both eyes!

   b. You increase your attention span and you begin to pick up important facial expressions of the speaker. (Smile, frown, downcast eyes, darting eye movements.)

c. You receive a *complete message* when the speaker's nonverbals *match* the content of her verbal message.

(She smiled and said, *"I'm happy you're feeling better."*)

d. You receive a *mixed message* when the speaker's nonverbals *do not match* the content of his verbal message.

(While obviously occupied with another task, he says to his secretary, *"I'm ready to discuss my travel agenda with you now."*)

e. You can control the conversation by establishing eye contact, asking clarifying questions, or restating what you are hearing. (If necessary, refer to PARAPHRASING TOOL, page 127.)

Dentist: *"We need a better plan for recalls."*

Manager: (While establishing direct eye contact) *"That sounds like a winner. What do you have in mind?"*
(Clarifying question)

(By asking this question, the manager controls the conversation.)

YOUR SPEAKER'S EYE BEHAVIORS:

a. You notice a speaker who *never* gives you eye contact when he or she responds to your questions. This eye behavior may be due to:
— Shyness or embarrassment.
— Learned response: "Never look someone straight in the eye."
— Belief in an ability to do two things at once.
— Belief in the fact that when you look someone in the eye, you give away some of your personal power (time, interest, or an ability to be controlled by the other.) Rather than giving away the power, the speaker chooses to *ignore your eyes.*

b. You notice a speaker who "stares a hole right through you."

(The speaker may simply be using your eyes as a focal point while his or her mind wanders on to other topics.)

c. You pick up various eye shifts of the speaker.

Know that the speaker is accessing sensory data from his or her memory and will use the data to verbally answer your question.
- His eyes may shift up to his left or right, accessing visual (picture) recall.
- His eyes may shift laterally, accessing auditory (sound) recall.
- His eyes may go down to his left or right, accessing emotional (sensation) recall.

(This information is based on the research of Richard Bandler and John Grinder. Their research is known as Neuro-Linguistic Programming [NLP]. Reference: *Frogs Into Princes*, published by Real People Press, Moab, Utah.)

5. Realize the fact that eyes generate more influential power than spoken words. So, stop what you're doing, look at the person's eyes and clear your mind for listening.

SITUATIONS:

- Conversing on a one-to-one basis in social and business settings.
- Listening to a person respond to your question and watching the way he or she accesses data.
- Wanting to reduce distractions while listening.
  (At the beginning of your conversation, eye contact may become a distraction until you are skilled in its use.)
- Interviewing purposes.
- Assessing a person's approach to buying something by observing his or her eye shifts.

- Selling products, ideas, etc., by listening to what the customer says. A customer might use one of these expressions:
  "I feel . . ."
  "I see . . ."
  "I hear . . ."

When you hear these expressions, respond with a matching message.

An Example

Customer: *"I need to see how it works."*

Your response: (While showing the customer a diagram)
"Look at this diagram and you'll see how each part works."

(You matched the customer's message.)

- Needing to control a conversation or discussion.

BENEFITS AND PAYOFFS:

1. Increases your attention span.

   (Research tells us that the average rate of speech is about 125 words a minute. The average person thinks at a rate nearly four times faster. Instead of allowing your mind to wander, you learn to focus your full attention on the speaker's eyes, the speaker's words and the speaker's nonverbals.)

2. Shows a speaker that you are interested in listening.

3. Attracts your full attention.

4. Conveys your attitude of caring about another person's thoughts, feelings and opinions.

5. Helps you overcome distractions such as paper shuffling, clock watching and phone dialing.

6. Allows you to practice empathetic listening.

7. Saves you time. You gain more information when you look while listening because you get the whole message, not just bits and pieces.

8. Develops your ability to evaluate how a person accesses sensory data to respond to your questions.

9. Sharpens your selling skills.

EXAMPLES OF PEOPLE USING THIS TOOL:

BUSINESS SETTING: Status Report Meeting

A subordinate briefs his boss on the status of a project. The supervisor knows she is allowing herself to be positively influenced by her subordinate when she gives her full eye attention to him.

(This supervisor wants to show her subordinate that she respects him for the time and effort he puts into his work. She also believes in listening with her eyes and her ears.)

* * *

BUSINESS SETTING: Counselor's Office

While *listening* to the client's problem, the counselor *notices* the client's eyes shifting frequently *down to her left*. The counselor knows that such a shift indicates the client is *accessing emotional experiences relating to her past*.

CAUTION:

DON'T keep your eyes focused on the other person's eyes for long periods of time.

Reason: Some people feel "stared at" and become intimidated. Often, such feelings result in self-defeating behaviors for these people. For instance, Rick's "undivided attention" on Pete's eyes unnerved Pete so much that he lost his train of thought and he began to ramble during his presentation.

DO deflect your eye focus about every 5-8 seconds by blinking or looking away. Then, return your focus immediately to regain the person's confidence in your ability to listen attentively.

TROUBLESHOOTING:

"I'm using this tool and it doesn't seem to work for me."

NATURE OF DIFFICULTY — Problem

"I'm having problems dealing with a doctor who requests briefings on meetings he can't make. When I begin to brief him, I notice that he's distracted by the paperwork that is in front of him. He continues to read his papers and I become annoyed at his behavior. It's impossible to focus my eyes on his as all I ever see is the top of his head. How do I get him to listen with his eyes as well as his ears?"

SUGGESTIONS:

A. Stop your briefing and allow the *silence* to get his attention. If he asks why you have stopped talking, simply say that you noticed it wasn't a good time to brief him as he seemed distracted.

B. Choose to make a self-disclosure statement.

   "Mr. Sims, I'm noticing that you need to do your paperwork right now. I'd like to reschedule our meeting so we can both concentrate on the same issue."

   Follow the self-disclosure statement with an open-ended question.

   "When would be a better time today?"

C. Assert yourself and ask if there is a reason why he doesn't look at you when he listens.

> **Option:** State the following:
>
> *"I'm having a problem speaking to you because I am not able to make any eye contact with you. Is this a 'bad time' for me to be meeting with you?"*

NOTE: ACCORDING TO STATISTICAL RESEARCH, 38% OF A PERSON'S LISTENING ATTENTION IS FOCUSED ON SUBVOCALS (PAUSES, EMPHASES, TONES), 55% ON NONVERBALS (FACIALS AND BODY MOVEMENTS), AND ONLY 7% ON SPOKEN WORDS. ALLOW THIS INFORMATION TO AFFECT THE MESSAGES YOU SEND AND THE WAY YOU RECEIVE OTHER PEOPLES' MESSAGES. LISTEN WITH YOUR EYES AND YOUR EARS! THIS IS A **TRADE SECRET.**

TOOL 12

FOGGING

DEFINITION:

A TOOL FOR "PUTTING PEOPLE OFF" FOR A TIME BY GIVING GENERAL OR NONCOMMITTAL ANSWERS TO THEIR QUESTIONS. LISTENERS USE THIS TOOL WHEN THEY CHOOSE TO RESPOND TO CRITICAL REMARKS MADE DIRECTLY TO THEM.

HOW THIS TOOL WORKS:

1. Listen to the question or to the critical remark.

2. Determine how you want to handle the matter.

   FOR QUESTIONS:

   a. Give general answers which contain vague or unaccountable data.

   An Example

   Alice: *"What's the status on Project M?"*

   You: *"We're working on it."*
   (Fogging response)

   b. Tell only what you need to tell! However, you need to be certain that what you say is *true*. Don't disclose precise or detailed positions on an issue if you don't need to. You have your reasons for not telling more. So don't!

   FOR CRITICAL REMARKS:

   a. Make a statement admitting your compliance or your agreement with a remark made to you since it could be true. Remember, your response must allow you to feel comfortable and "in charge" of yourself.

An Example

Ron: *"You spent too much time redoing those portfolio sketches, Al."*
(Critical remark)

Al: *"You're probably right, Ron."*
(Fogging response)

b. Respond only to what is said, not to what is meant! However, you need to be certain that what you say *could probably be true.* You do not need to *explain, defend or allow yourself to be manipulated.* You're still "in charge" of your healthy self-esteem. Besides, you are the ultimate judge of your actions.

c. **Option Step:** If you want to know the intended meaning of a critical remark made to you, ask a clarifying question after you make your fogging response.

An Example

Ron: *"You spent too much time redoing those portfolio sketches, Al."*
(Critical remark)

Al: *"You're probably right, Ron.*
(Fogging response)

But what makes you say that, Ron?"
(Clarifying question)

3. Develop a list of fogging responses for quick recall when situations demand such responses. (See List of Examples, page 83 .)

SITUATIONS:
- Dealing with people who put you "on the spot."
- Confronting questions or remarks which require more data than you wish to give.

- Resisting manipulative-type people.
- Handling a negative comment for something you did.
- Looking at yourself with a critical and healthy eye.

BENEFITS AND PAYOFFS:

Using Fogging Responses to Questions

1. Allows you to verbalize a degree of accountability by telling the person, *"We're working on it."*

2. Protects your current information which lacks precision and specific detail. An example: *"We'll call you when it's ready."*

3. Sends a message to your questioner that you did hear his remark.

4. Permits you to respond when you're *in a bind*.

Using Fogging Responses to Critical Remarks

1. Gives you some leeway in responding to *demanding situations*.

2. Helps you maintain an *okay posture* when your prior conditioning has said, *"Get angry and be defensive."*

3. Desensitizes you to hearing and coping with heavy negativity directed towards you.

4. Gives you an opportunity to agree with your critic.

EXAMPLES OF PEOPLE USING THIS TOOL:

Fogging Responses to Questions
— *"Maybe."*
— *"That's interesting."*
— *"Next week."*
— *"It's on order."*
— *"I'll call you."*
— *"We'll see."*
— *"We've always done it this way."*

Fogging Responses to Critical Remarks
- *"That's probably true."*
- *"I'm sure it is."*
- *"It sounds fair."*
- *"You may be right."*
- *"That's very probable."*
- *"Sounds like you may be right."*
- *"That's a good point."*
- *"I can see where you could think that about me."*
- *"Perhaps."*

CAUTION:

DON'T use fogging remarks when your situation demands *on-line* and *front-end* answers. Be advised: It is not wise to play games with peoples' heads. Such a perception could occur if you were to use fogging responses, repeatedly, with the same person.

Reason: Some people may believe that you are *incapable of giving a precise answer when such an answer is necessary.* They may also judge you as incompetent!

DO use these tools when you are able to handle the consequences involved in their use. Some communication behaviors of certain people require you to confront them with this Tool.

TROUBLESHOOTING:

"I'm using this tool and it doesn't seem to work for me."

NATURE OF DIFFICULTY — Problem

"My supervisor is having some trouble with the fiscal director. Yesterday, my supervisor asked me how I got along with the fiscal department. I said, *'Fine.'* But my supervisor keeps after me and I don't want to get involved. So, what do I do?"

SUGGESTIONS:

A. Make the remark, *"I have no comment on the matter, Ben."* He may say, *"Oh, you never reveal your feelings about anything that goes on around here."* With that critical remark, you might wish to agree with him as there does seem to be an element of truth to what he says. Your response: *"You may be right about that, Ben."*

B. With either comment you make, you will not be dishonest in your statements. This is the key to gaining expertise in the use of this Tool.

C. Use the DEFOGGING TOOL, page 59, for additional help in coping with Ben.

NOTE: FOGGING RESPONSES WORK IN SPECIFIC SITUATIONS, SO YOU'LL WANT TO HANDLE THIS TOOL WITH DISCRETION. AT THIS POINT, YOU ARE AWARE OF FOGGERS AND FOGGING DEVICES. YOU POSSESS A **TRADE SECRET!**

TOOL 13

GIVING FEEDBACK

DEFINITION:

A TOOL FOR GIVING EVALUATIVE INPUT TO AN INDIVIDUAL OR GROUP ON ONE OR MORE OF THEIR BEHAVIORS. USERS OF THIS TOOL TELL INDIVIDUALS OR GROUP MEMBERS HOW THEIR SPECIFIC BEHAVIORS ARE AFFECTING THEIR WORK PERFORMANCES AS WELL AS CERTAIN PEOPLE WHO COME IN CONTACT WITH THEM.

HOW THIS TOOL WORKS:

1. Consider your purpose in wanting to give feedback to the individual or group.

   HERE'S HOW:

   "He's losing his audience by his long-winded responses to their questions. I want the group to listen to him and to value what he says."

2. Consider the readiness of the individual to receive the feedback. Use self-talk!

   HERE'S AN EXAMPLE OF SELF-TALK:

   "I think he respects me enough to listen to what I have to say to him."

3. Use the person's name and state your need.

   HERE'S HOW:

   "Corry, I need to give you some feedback on the discussion that occurred during the staff meeting this morning."

4. Ask the person if he would like to hear what you have to say.

HERE'S HOW:

"Corry, would you like to hear my comments?"

a. If he says *"No,"* do not give your feedback at this time. Wait or just skip this Step and continue with Step #6.

(Be aware that you may not have a listener if you skip this Step!)

b. If he says *"Yes,"* continue!

5. Give your specific feedback when you get a *"Yes"* response to Step #4.

6. Focus your comments on observable behaviors; what *you have seen or heard*.

BEGIN THIS WAY:

"Corry, I listened and noticed that your response . . ."

DO NOT BEGIN WITH THIS PHRASE:

"Corry, you shouldn't . . ."

(This phrase indicts him!)

7. *Send matching messages!* Your nonverbal and verbal expressions need to say the same thing!

Be sure your facial gestures and the rest of your body convey the same constructive message as your words.

8. Check with the person, after giving your feedback, to see if he or she received your intended message.

HERE'S HOW:

"Corry, what are you hearing me say?"

9. Explore alternative behaviors with the person when he or she has accepted your feedback.

HERE'S HOW:

"What are some other ways of responding to people's questions without turning them off, Corry?"

10. Give feedback on positive behavior too!

    (Use the above Steps #1-7 or see the TOOL on CREDITING, page 45, for additional help.)

SITUATIONS:

- Confronting a person whose behavior during meetings is unacceptable.
- Crediting a worker for a job well done.
- Conducting performance review sessions.
- Facilitating team-building sessions which involve teaching people how to "level" with each other.
- Improving morale in an office setting.
- Dealing with interpersonal problems involving family members.
- Coping with an employee who "turns off" customers. (The employee is not aware that her actions convey negative messages to customers.)
- Listening to people who repeat their stories or give you too much data on a given point.
- Working with trainees, co-workers, neighbors, etc. who do things *differently* from you or others.

BENEFITS AND PAYOFFS:

1. Helps you conduct a professional performance appraisal session with ratings based on documented, observable behaviors rather than personality traits.

2. Provides you with an opportunity to *self-disclose*.

   (In self-disclosure, you tell a person how you see things and how you feel about what you see.)

3. Keeps you "on track" and able to confront crises situations.

4. Gives your people information they can choose to use or not to use.

5. Helps your people become aware of what they do not know about themselves.

6. Allows you to correct or adjust meanings that are received erroneously by the person getting your feedback.

7. Equips you with a procedure or formula for giving feedback. Eliminates the "shooting from the hip" approach.

8. Empowers you to control discussions which tend to move away from the stated topic.

9. Allows you to use the PARAPHRASING TOOL for insuring communication accuracy.

10. Saves money and time by eliminating "avoidance tactics" from your management style.

EXAMPLES OF PEOPLE USING THIS TOOL:

(Feedback used to check communication accuracy.)

Cindy: *"Ernie, I need to let you know that I've been covering your floor duty for the past two nights. When you don't arrive at the Nurse's Station, I have to extend my time to cover for you. What's been making you late each night?"*

Ernie: *"I could say it's been traffic or lots of things. Really, Cindy, I just don't leave home early enough. But what I hear you saying is that you would like to go off duty at your assigned time, right?"*

Cindy: *"Right!"*

(Ernie got her exact message.)

* * *

(Feedback directed toward behavior rather than the person.)

Joe: *"I felt you talked for a long time this afternoon, Bill."*

(Feedback directed at Bill's behavior.)

vs.

Joe: *"Bill, you're a loud mouth. Did you know that?"*

(Feedback directed at the total person.)

* * *

(Feedback that is specific rather than general.)

Barry: *"When Paula was telling you about her accident last night, you interrupted her four times."*

(Feedback is specific.)

vs.

Barry: *"You are aggressive, Jim."*

(Feedback is too general. Barry needs to direct his feedback toward a specific situation.)

* * *

(Feedback that is complimentary.)

Marcia: *"Ken, I think you did an excellent job on the report you gave in the front office today. Thanks."*

(Feedback gives credit where it is due!)

CAUTION:

DON'T fall into the trap of using the familiar pronoun "We" when giving your feedback.

Reason: Some people will use the pronoun "We" in giving feedback because they do not want to individually own the data or be blamed for the content and effects of their statements. Others will use "We" when they lack confidence in what they are saying. So, they *"mask"* their insecurity by using this pronoun. Most people who receive this type of feedback devalue it, since the source of the feedback is vague!

DO use the personal pronoun "I" when giving your feedback and let others speak for themselves! Use your own observable data and share your feelings and your reactions to the other person's behavior. Then, you are *solely responsible* for giving specific examples to help the person understand the meaning of your feedback.

TROUBLESHOOTING:

"I'm using this tool and it doesn't seem to work for me."

NATURE OF DIFFICULTY — Problem

"While talking on the phone, I gave some unsolicited feedback to Sharon about the way she handled the breakdown of one of the city buses. I thought I used all the correct language. Well, she snapped back at me with some strong, vulgar words! Where did I go wrong?"

SUGGESTIONS:

A. Review your reason for giving her your feedback. Giving unsolicited feedback is risky! Nevertheless, if your purpose is to help — use all the Steps listed in the Section, HOW THIS TOOL WORKS, page 87. Be sure your feedback is well-timed. See Step #4 to insure correct timing.

B. Watch your tone when giving your feedback. Research tells us that in the communication process, 55% of the impact of our message deals with non-verbals, 38% deals with subvocals (pauses, emphases, tones) and only 7% deals with the spoken word. Perhaps *the worst way for Sharon to get feedback is by phone!*

C. Ask for restatement after giving your feedback. I'm not sure Sharon heard your message accurately. She heard a message! She didn't necessarily hear yours! This may be the source of your problem.

NATURE OF DIFFICULTY — Problem

"I've got a boss who seems to delight in making caustic remarks to his staff members. No matter what we do, he always finds something in our work to pick apart. How do I initiate a feedback session with him?"

SUGGESTIONS:

A. Ask him for a ten minute meeting in his office. Then, explain your reason for wanting to meet with him and ask him if he would like to pursue the matter.

B. If you get a *"Yes"* response, continue.

(If you get a *"No"* response, stop. Negotiate for another time.)

NOTE: FEEDBACK IS AN ESSENTIAL ELEMENT IN ANY CONTROL PROCESS. THIS PROCESS CAN BE FOUND IN THE STUDIES OF SPACE RESEARCH, PHOTOGRAPHY, COMPUTER SCIENCE AND THE BEHAVIORAL SCIENCES. HANDLE THIS TOOL WITH EXTREME SENSITIVITY AS IT SERVES TO INCREASE AWARENESS, PRECISION AND ACCURACY AMONG THOSE WHO USE IT AND THOSE WHO RECEIVE IT. NOW YOU KNOW WHY THIS TOOL IS A **TRADE SECRET!**

TOOL 14
HOOK QUESTIONS

DEFINITION:

A TOOL FOR GETTING PEOPLE TO ANSWER "YES" TO YOUR QUESTIONS. USERS OF THIS PERSUASION TOOL ASK LOADED QUESTIONS WHICH USUALLY REQUIRE A "YES" OR AN AGREEABLE RESPONSE FROM THEIR LISTENERS. LOADED QUESTIONS CONTAIN *HIDDEN* OR *NOT-SO-HIDDEN* OPINIONS OF THEIR USERS.

HOW THIS TOOL WORKS:

1. Begin with a hook-stem phrase such as:

   "Don't you think . . ."

   "Isn't it true . . ."

   "Haven't you ever thought . . ."

   "Wouldn't it be true to say . . ."

   "Can't you understand that . . ."

2. Inject your opinion after the hook-stem phrase.

   "Don't you think that some employees' ideas are valuable?"

   "Isn't it true that the speaker should follow her outline more closely?"

3. Use a questioning tone to let the listener know that you are expecting an answer. Also, give a little *nod of your head* to reinforce the idea that you are expecting a "Yes" answer.

4. Wait for the listener to say, *"Yes."*

Speaker: *"Don't you think some employees' ideas are valuable?"*

Listener: *"Yes, I certainly do."*

(At this point you have successfully "hooked" the listener into agreeing with you.)

HERE ARE THE KEY ELEMENTS

Hook Stem Phrase + Your Opinion + Questioning Tone = "Yes" Response

---

5. Variations:

   a. Give your opinion. Then, use a hook-stem phrase.

      Speaker: *"You really like your new office,*
      (Opinion)
      don't you?"
      (Hook-stem phrase)

      Listener: *"Yes, I do."*

   b. Develop your opinion in such a way that makes your listener respond with a "No." You are really hooking the listener into agreeing with you.

      Speaker: *"You don't know when he'll be back,*
      (Opinion)
      do you?"
      (Hook-stem phrase)

      Listener: *"No, I don't."*
      (You expected this answer)

   (At this point you have successfully "hooked" the listener into agreeing with you.)

HERE ARE THE KEY ELEMENTS

Your Opinion + Hook Stem Phrase + Questioning Tone = "No" Response

---

SITUATIONS:

- Selling your ideas, products, services, points of view.
- Seeking quick agreements on your opinions.
- Reducing tension in some of your conflict situations by allowing yourself to act as a peace maker.
- Persuading some of your people to do what you want them to do or need them to do.
- Attracting a person's attention. Most people like to be asked for their advice. By asking Hook Questions, you seek the listener's agreement on your advice.

BENEFITS AND PAYOFFS:

1. Presents your opinion without sounding egotistical.

2. Gives you an affirmative response to your questions.

3. Gets people to *"buy in"* to your sales pitch at an early stage.

4. Gives you an opportunity to gain support for your opinions.

5. Empowers you and your group members to end a discussion or meeting on the "upbeat."

   She said, *"Don't you think it's time to end this meeting?"*

6. Influences some of your people to think positively.

7. Stimulates your people to feel good about answering questions with a "Yes" response. Many people like to give "Yes" answers rather than "No" answers.

EXAMPLES OF PEOPLE USING THIS TOOL:

SOCIAL SETTING

(A house guest comments on the new wallpaper in her friend's kitchen.)

97

Guest: *"Doesn't it look beautiful?"*
(Hook Question)

Friend: *"Yes, I like it, too."*
(Agreement)

* * *

BUSINESS SETTING: Performance Appraisals

Supervisor A: *"Isn't it true that performance appraisals are more beneficial when both parties agree on their ratings?"*
(Hook Question)

Supervisor B: *"Yes, I think that's true."*
(Agreement)

* * *

BUSINESS SETTING: Time Clocks

Warehouse
Employee: *"Haven't you wondered why time clocks are rarely punched by middle and upper management?"*
(Hook Question)

Warehouse
Janitor: *"Yeah, but I don't spend my nights thinking about it!"*
(Agreement)

* * *

BUSINESS SETTING: Staff Meetings

Office Manager: *"You don't really want to miss another staff meeting, do you?"*
(Hook Question)

Staff Member: *"Of course not!"*
(Agreement)

CAUTION:

DON'T use Hook Questions indiscreetly! Sometimes, you'll want to ask a direct or open-ended question because some people do not like to answer Hook Questions.

Reason: Some people feel manipulated and angry when asked loaded questions by so-called *communication experts.* These people feel like they have been "backed into a corner." They prefer more open and less threatening types of questions.

DO ask a Hook Question when you intend to influence the responder to view an issue from your point of view. However, when you intend to get the responder's viewpoint first, ask another type of question. (See OPEN-ENDED QUESTIONS, page 9.)

TROUBLESHOOTING:

"I'm using this tool and it doesn't seem to work for me."

NATURE OF DIFFICULTY — Problem

"When I asked a co-worker a Hook Question, he surprised me with a "No" answer. I couldn't believe it! What went wrong?"

SUGGESTIONS:

A. Be aware that a listener always has the right to answer a question any way he or she wants. Your listener did not agree with your opinion. He responded with a "No" and he meant it. Most people do not listen as acutely as your friend. However, there are some people who may honestly agree with an opinion. So they respond with a "Yes" and they do not feel *hooked* by the questioner.

B. Ask your friend a clarifying question regarding his "No" answer.

"Why did you say 'No' to my question?"

Watch your tone, otherwise he may not wish to say anything.

C. If you are not interested in why your friend said "No," then simply accept his answer.

NATURE OF DIFFICULTY — Problem

"I'm now aware of asking people Hook Questions when I don't intend to. How do I stop myself from asking the question when it's already out of my mouth?"

SUGGESTIONS:

A. Stop in the middle of the question or rephrase the entire question after you ask it.

"Don't you think that coffee breaks . . ."

(Stop and rephrase your question into an Open-Ended Question.)

"What is your opinion of . . ."

(See OPEN-ENDED QUESTIONS TOOL, page 9.)

B. Start off by stating your opinion. Then ask the other person for his or hers.

"I think coffee breaks are good for building positive morale. What do you think?"

(See OPEN-ENDED QUESTIONS TOOL, page 9.)

NATURE OF DIFFICULTY — Problem

"I need to know how to respond to Hook Questions."

SUGGESTIONS:

A. First, realize that some people use Hook Questions accidently or unintentionally because they may not feel comfortable expressing their direct opinion. They prefer to camouflage their opinion into a Hook Question. For instance, when a person states her opinion directly, she would say:

"I think staff meetings are boring."

If this person states her opinion indirectly, she would say:

"Don't you think that staff meetings are boring?"

Some people have been conditioned not to use the pronoun "I" when *they speak their mind*. They feel that a Hook Question is more acceptable, so they express their opinion in this manner. Most people do not realize they are "hooking" their listeners into agreeing with them.

B. Respond to a Hook Question by:

— Asking the person an Open-Ended Question.

"What do you think of staff meetings, Terry?"

— Asking the person a Hook Question.

"Don't you think staff meetings are boring, Terry?"

— Answering the person's question honestly.

"Yes" or *"No."*

NOTE: BE AWARE OF ASKING AND RESPONDING TO HOOK OR LOADED QUESTIONS. AWARE-NESS IS THE KEY! WHEN YOU ARE AWARE OF WHAT YOU SAY, YOU ARE IN CONTROL! YOU POSSESS A **TRADE SECRET**.

TOOL 15

INNER POWER

DEFINITION:

A TOOL WHICH HELPS PEOPLE RELEASE POSITIVE
ENERGY FROM THEIR *INNER SELVES* FOR PRODUCTIVE
PAYOFFS. USERS OF THIS TOOL DEVELOP AN AWARENESS
OF THEIR POWER POTENTIAL BY LEARNING TO PROGRAM
THEIR SUBCONSCIOUS MIND.

HOW THIS TOOL WORKS:

1. Recognize and consciously admit that you want to work with your conscious and subconscious mind.

2. Prepare yourself for this work by reviewing the functions of your mind.

   Your Conscious Mind
   - Initiates thoughts.
   - Collects and analyzes data.
   - Directs and controls your actions.
   - Generates energy.

   * * *

   Your Subconscious Mind
   - Receives directions from the conscious.
   - Retains directions and builds associations from past and present data to accomplish its assigned task.
   - Creates, imagines, visualizes and produces your decisions.
   - Generates energy.

   * * *

Synergistic Effect

Since the subconscious works on the directions it receives from the conscious, the subconscious does its best work when its directions are logical, clear and specific. So, you may want to write or verbalize your directions before asking your subconscious to *"take over."*

3. Program your subconscious when you feel relaxed.

(Your conscious mind is inactive at this time so your subconscious *"goes to work"* without distraction from your conscious mind.)

4. Do this programming by yourself. This is strictly *your business*.

HERE'S HOW TO DO IT:

a. Direct your subconscious to work out your plan, desire or problem. Since you are interested in results, leave the method to your subconscious.

b. Reinforce your request. Also, do as much "groundwork" as necessary.

(Your subconscious works on what you give it to work on!)

c. Make verbal affirmations, in writing or in your conscious mind, to support the work your subconscious is doing.

An Affirmation

"I expect my subconscious to work out a solution. I have confidence in my subconscious. I will continue to search for better data so it can do its best job for me."

d. Withdraw and let your subconscious *work*. Your answer will come in the form of a solution or in a method to arrive at a solution.

e. Evaluate your answer with your conscious mind. Choose to use or not to use the answer.

(See the *Wisdom of Your Subconscious Mind*, by John K. Williams for reference.)

SITUATIONS:

- Finding the best way to sell a product or a service.
- Overcoming negative thinking in all its forms.
- Preparing for an initial or exit interview.
- Coping with difficult people.
- Eliminating the desire to make judgmental remarks about people.
- Dealing with sickness.
- Wishing to accomplish realistic goals.
- Changing a behavior pattern or getting rid of a bad habit.

BENEFITS AND PAYOFFS:

1. Shows you how to develop a sense of wholeness because you have a method for coping with anything, and you are at peace with your inner self.

2. Activates the untapped potential of your mind.

3. Utilizes new energy sources allowing you to creatively manage your day.

4. Provides you with tools for handling criticism, stress, and low self-esteem in yourself or others.

5. Helps you to acquire a healthy outlook toward routine matters or crises situations.

6. Equips you to function as a change agent for people who need tools to cope with everyday living.

7. Empowers you to take charge of your life and make of life what you will. No excuses allowed! You are in touch with the power of your subconscious.

EXAMPLES OF PEOPLE USING THIS TOOL:

FAMILY SETTING: Dental Appointment

(Terry needs to have three wisdom teeth extracted next month. He decides to program his subconscious to help him deal with this ordeal. He says:)

"I've got to get these teeth out. The X-rays show they are not impacted. Thank God! Okay, subconscious, I've done my 'groundwork.' Help me cope with this ordeal."

Terry withdraws his attention from the matter and lets his subconscious go to work.

In the meantime, he makes verbal affirmations and he reinforces his feelings of confidence in his subconscious. He believes in his inner powers! His dental appointment goes well. He is *in control* and he feels relaxed. He is a "together" person!

* * *

BUSINESS SETTING: Selling Real Estate

A realtor needs to deal with a client who constantly sees the *negative side* of things. The realtor is ready to "throw in the towel" and let another firm handle her client. As a last resort, the realtor begins to work with her subconscious.

To give her subconscious the best set of directions;

— she visualizes the steps she has taken,

— she asks her subconscious to give her a solution,

— she is relaxed and alone.

She begins: *"Subconscious, direct me toward a solution for dealing with this client. I'm leaving it in your hands. I know we'll be able to deal better with my client's negativity."*

A few days later, she gets some "hunches." She decides to use them. They work! She uses her Inner Power.

CAUTION:

DON'T send *mixed directions* to your subconscious and then expect to get clear and precise answers.

Case-in-Point

After a bridge party, you hear yourself making these comments about one of the members:

"I can't stand her remarks. They hurt and I feel terrible. There is no way we will ever hit it off. Subconscious, fix this situation for me. Make it work!"

(First, you admit there is no way anything will happen. Then you order your subconscious to fix it up. You are sending *mixed directions* to your subconscious.)

Reason: Your subconscious works on the data you give it. When you send mixed messages — like the above — your subconscious can not effectively work for you, because you do not clearly tell it what you want. You have produced a mental conflict for your subconscious and the conflict will show up in the way you begin to feel — anxious, guilty and lacking a sense of direction.

DO remember that the conscious and subconscious must agree. Otherwise the subconscious gets mixed impressions on what you want to happen. To avoid such confusion, make affirmations like:

"My mind is clear. Although I'm upset by some comments I heard, I want to be able to cope better for my good and her good. Go to work subconscious; we're on the same wave length."

Now, you have involved your conscious and subconscious mind in a clear, cooperative effort to manage the situation.

TROUBLESHOOTING:

"I'm using this tool and it doesn't seem to work for me."

NATURE OF DIFFICULTY — Problem

"Before going to sleep one night, I told my subconscious to wake me up at 6:45 a.m. Now, I also told myself that this wouldn't work. How could it! Imagine, telling myself to wake myself up. I gave it a try but I set my alarm just in case. The alarm woke me up as I figured it would. Why didn't my subconscious do its work?"

SUGGESTIONS:

A. Think about what you have just said. You will see why your subconscious "didn't do its work."

You told your subconscious to wake you up. Then you immediately denied your own order. ("I told myself this wouldn't work.") You placed your subconscious in a state of mental confusion and your subconscious worked on your most dominant thought. ("I told myself this wouldn't work — so I'm setting the alarm.")

B. Believe in what you say. Then reinforce that belief with affirmations. Expect your subconscious to work on clearly given orders! You have a "built-in" alarm clock if you would only believe you do.

C. Review the Steps in the Section: HOW THIS TOOL WORKS, page 103.

NOTE: AN OPEN-MINDED PERSON IS WILLING TO CONSIDER NEW FACTS. HERE ARE THREE NEW FACTS FOR SOME OF YOU.

1) YOUR SUBCONSCIOUS MIND IS YOUR INNER POWER. ARE YOU WILLING TO CONSIDER USING IT?

2) YOUR SUBCONSCIOUS IS ALWAYS WORKING FOR YOU BUT IT WORKS BETTER WHEN *YOU* DIRECT ITS WORK. ARE YOU WILLING TO DIRECT ITS WORK?

3) YOU ARE WHAT YOU THINK! IF YOU THINK YOU'RE POWERFUL — YOU ARE!

TO UNDERSTAND HOW YOUR INNER POWER WORKS IS TO UNDERSTAND A **TRADE SECRET**.

TOOL 16

LEGITIMIZING A MEMBER'S PRESENCE OR ABSENCE AT MEETINGS

DEFINITION:

A TOOL WHICH RECOGNIZES AND AFFIRMS THE VALUE OF A MEMBER'S PRESENCE OR ABSENCE AT A MEETING. USERS OF THIS TOOL TELL MEETING ATTENDEES THE STATUS OF EACH INVITED MEMBER, SINCE IT IS THEIR RIGHT TO KNOW.

HOW THIS TOOL WORKS:

1. Become aware of a *group dynamics principle* that states:

   Group members have specific rights and procedures for handling the presence and absence of invited members at meetings.

2. Acknowledge the presence of each member and legitimize the absence of any member at the *beginning* of all meetings.

   HERE'S HOW TO DO IT:

   a. Express appreciation for the presence of attending members and legitimize the presence of those persons representing invited members. Mention each representative by name and function.

   b. Give the reason why each absent member is not present. If a reason is confidential, say, *"Joan Engel will not be attending today's meeting. Something has come to her immediate attention and she needs to deal with it."*

3. Allow other members to offer their comments and reasons for absent members, if you have not been advised as to their non-attendance.

   HERE'S HOW TO DO IT:

   a. Simply legitimize the fact that some members are not present, and ask members if they have any information that could explain the absence of these members.

   b. Give time for the sharing of this information.

4. Use this same procedure (See Step #3) for dealing with *late arrivals*. Be careful not to repeat detailed information for the *late arrival*. However, be sure to welcome this person.

   (Use a nod of your head or a greeting word.)

5. Take about 10 seconds to use this Tool.

6. Train invited members to legitimize their absences prior to the scheduled meeting by informing their chairperson or another attending member. (This process involves all members regardless of rank and position within the group or organization.)

SITUATIONS:

- Building a work group into a team. Members begin to feel responsible and accountable for their participation or lack of participation in the group.

- Improving positive morale among people of all ranks. When you tell attending members why some members are absent, you give all members an opportunity to relate on a non-ranked basis. Information is power and sharing this information (peoples' whereabouts) lets people participate in your power on a non-ranked basis.

- Starting a conference, meeting or session. Usually at the start-up of a meeting, some members look around to see who is present and who is not present. If these members are not rightfully informed about another member's absence, they may be distracted through the entire meeting. So, tell present members, at the beginning of your meeting, the whereabouts of absent members.

BENEFITS AND PAYOFFS:

1. Builds better rapport with staff members because you share information which is often equated with sharing your power.

2. Improves the quality of input from participants in the meeting since they are aware of the reasons for some members' absences. Now, attending members will not spend their time *assuming* why some people are not present.

3. Provides opportunity to use genuine, group dynamics skills in an effort to run effective and efficient meetings.

4. Produces results-oriented meeting behaviors from present and absent members, since all members will be exercising proactive, accountable skills.

5. Reduces and ultimately eliminates embarrassment that persons-in-charge feel when they are "in the dark" regarding one or more members who do not show up for a scheduled meeting.

6. Enables participants to understand and act on their responsibilities.

EXAMPLES OF PEOPLE USING THIS TOOL:

BUSINESS SETTING

Chairperson: *"Marilyn will not be at our meeting today. She is chairing a panel on 'Nutritional Needs for Diabetics.'"*

(Legitimizing invited member's absence.)

* * *

BUSINESS SETTING

Project
Manager:
"*Thank you for attending the meeting and allowing us to start on time. I need you to know that Mr. Lyons will not be present. He will be in Washington. Mr. Lyons has sent Mr. Duffy to represent him. Mr. Duffy is chief liaison to Mr. Lyons. Welcome, Mr. Duffy.*"

(Legitimizing a member's absence and acknowledging the presence of their representative by name and function.)

* * *

BUSINESS SETTING

Chairperson:
"*I'd like to start our meeting. I see that John and Glen are not here. I am not aware of any reason for their absence. Can anyone help me out?*"

Member:
"*Yes, Glen told me he was not feeling well and to let you know he wouldn't be coming today.*"

(Member had forgotten to share this information with the Chair prior to the meeting.)

Chairperson:
"*Thanks. What about John?*"

Member:
"*On my way over I saw John talking with the Chief. I have a feeling he'll be late.*"

Chairperson:
"*Thanks. If John doesn't show, I'll let you know what happened at our next meeting. Let's begin with the first agenda item.*"

(Other members give reasons why certain members are not present. The Tool works!)

CAUTION:

DON'T assume that invited members at a meeting *"could care less"* why other invited members are not present at the meeting. Likewise, don't assume that rank and position excuse some people from having to legitimize their absences.

Reason: Most people are curious by nature! They want to know where "Person X" is. If they aren't told, they start making up their own reasons during the meeting. Now, these same members are supposed to be listening and actively participating in your agenda. However, they do not give you their *full attention* because they are distracted, and you do not receive their quality input!

DO become skilled in group dynamics principles. Begin to legitimize members' presences and absences at the start of your meetings. Allow your members full access to information that is rightfully theirs! Give them every opportunity to contribute their best to each agenda point. Give them *no opportunity to make assumptions as to why some people are not at the meeting.*

TROUBLESHOOTING:

"I'm using this tool and it doesn't seem to work for me."

NATURE OF DIFFICULTY — Problem

"We never know who is supposed to attend some of our meetings. We just know when we're supposed to be there. How can we get the chairperson to tell us who has been invited?"

SUGGESTIONS:

A. Ask the chairperson to send a memo indicating the names of invited members (copies to: _ _ _ _ _). The Chain-of-Command can distribute this memo prior to the actual meeting.

B. When the meeting begins, ask if there is anyone missing from the scheduled list of invited members. This proactive behavior of yours ought to stimulate the chairperson, or others, to legitimize the reasons for absent members. Any group member has the right to ask for this information! This type of behavior helps attendees to *"sense"* that this meeting is their meeting and not *just* the chairperson's meeting.

NATURE OF DIFFICULTY — Problem

"When certain supervisors are absent from my meetings, I ask their department head for a reason. He says he doesn't know where they are and acts like he doesn't care. What do I do?"

SUGGESTIONS:

A. Talk with him after your meeting. Tell him his credibility is "on the line." This non-caring attitude will soon cost him the respect of his other line supervisors.

B. Ask him to send a memo to all his supervisors informing them of their need to legitimize their presence, lateness or absence at scheduled meetings.

NOTE: IF YOU HAVE NOT BEEN USING THIS TOOL CONSISTENTLY, START NOW! YOU WILL SEE A DIFFERENCE IN THE QUALITY OF INPUT YOU WILL RECEIVE FROM YOUR PRESENT GROUP MEMBERS. WHY? BECAUSE THEY KNOW YOU CARE ABOUT THEM AND YOU CARE ABOUT WHAT THEY HAVE TO OFFER. IT'S A **"TRADE SECRET!"**

TOOL 17

MANAGING AND RESOLVING PROBLEMS

DEFINITION:

A TOOL WHICH HELPS SOME PEOPLE CONFRONT, MANAGE AND RESOLVE THEIR PROBLEMS. THIRD PARTY RESOLVERS ALSO USE THIS TOOL TO SOLVE INTERPERSONAL PROBLEMS INVOLVING OTHER PEOPLE.

HOW THIS TOOL WORKS:

1. Use the *Problem Identification Form*, page   , to identify the essential elements of a problem situation.

2. Analyze the situation for these points:
   a. What is the problem?
   b. Who owns the problem?
   c. What type of problem is it — one-way or two-way?
   d. Are you able to accurately express the problem to the person's satisfaction or to each person's satisfaction?

   An Example

   (You are the third party. Cindy and Barb are the involved parties in this problem situation. Cindy owns the problem.)

   Third Party: *"Cindy, you say you're having a problem coping with the impending office move that Barb informed you about this morning. Right?"*

> Cindy: *"Yes. You've got my feelings exactly."*
>
> Barb: *"I didn't know you were having a problem with it, Cindy."*

3. Continue to develop the parameters of the problem by asking clarifying questions of both parties. (See OPEN-ENDED QUESTIONS TOOL, page 9, Steps #2 and #3.)

4. Request that both parties restate the problem in its entirety even though only one party owns the problem.

   (This process guarantees that each party has been heard.)

5. Allow each party to suggest ways to solve the problem. Have each party ask appropriate questions of the other:

   HERE'S HOW:

   — *"What do you suggest I do to resolve my problem?"* (Problem owner's question.)

   — *"What do you suggest I do to help you resolve your problem?"* (Involved party's question.)

   List all suggestions. Frequently, one of the suggested answers to the above questions contains the resolution to the problem.

6. Allow both parties to select their best option.

   Criterion: Best option needs to satisfy both parties.

7. Get each party to formulate an Action Plan.

   ELEMENTS OF AN ACTION PLAN:

   a. There needs to be a new behavior or an agreed-upon action for resolving the problem. (Such behavior needs to be written in a statement format containing specific, measurable terms.)

   b. There needs to be a feedback procedure for monitoring progress.

   (This procedure needs to contain dates, times and places for carrying out the Plan.)

8. Recognize the fact that *some problems are not resolvable, but all problems are manageable.*

SITUATIONS:

- Acting as a change agent when two or more persons are in conflict.
- Confronting another person with whom *you* are having a problem. (Use this procedure and wear *two hats*. Wear *one hat* as a third party resolver and wear *one hat* as a problem owner.)
- Suggesting this procedure when persons are unable to manage or resolve their problems.
- Rechanneling negative energies which result when people "attack" each other with their blame messages.
- Instructing others in learning a systematic approach for managing problems.

BENEFITS AND PAYOFFS:

1. Empowers you because you possess the right tool and you use it at the right time.

2. Focuses your mind on problem management rather than focusing your mind on just the problem.

3. Motivates you to confront difficult persons whose behaviors cause problems for you and others. Instead of complaining about their actions, you confront them with a procedure that works!

4. Gives you a *road map* for settling disputes.

5. Helps you eliminate procrastination and avoidance-type behaviors which are often used by people who do not like to confront their problems.

6. Helps you discern how to best use your skills when helping troubled people.

117

7. Equips you with basic problem resolution tools for improving interpersonal relationships involving yourself or other people.

EXAMPLES OF PEOPLE USING THIS TOOL:

Questions to ask when you need to determine problem owner(s):

— *"Who is upset?"*

— *"Who is bothered by the situation?"*

(If you have answered "I am" to the above questions, then the problem is probably yours. If you have answered "Someone else" or "Others" and they own it, then the problem is theirs.)

Questions to ask when you are functioning in the role of a Third Party resolver.

— *"Why are you upset with the situation?"*

— *"What are you doing or what have you done to let the other person know that his or her actions were really getting to you?"*

— *"What would you like this person to do differently?"*

CAUTION:

DON'T expect people to readily admit ownership of their problems. Said another way: Don't expect *finger pointers* to quickly become *finger owners.*

Reason: Many people tend to see or place blame for their problems on other people. Some people are not aware that their behaviors cause problems for other people. *We do not see ourselves as others see us and we do not know what we do not know.* So, some of us need to be told which of our behaviors are problem-causing for others. Some of us need to own the way we feel. Finger pointing doesn't accomplish anything!

DO work to properly identify the problem in yourself or others. Shy away from placing blame on anyone else. Most people will not accept blame!

TROUBLESHOOTING:

"I'm using this tool and it doesn't seem to work for me."

NATURE OF DIFFICULTY — Problem

"Here's my problem. Anne, Jack and I are partners in business. Anne doesn't take her responsibilities seriously. Here's a typical example: It's Anne's day to answer the phones. Already, she's missed three calls. Jack has had to cover for her before. Nothing seems to bother Anne. So, she misses a few calls here and there. She knows someone will always answer the phone and she's right! Someone like Jack will. Well, things are changing! Jack has had it with her! So have I! I know I have to confront her and I know I can use this tool, but I'm not sure of my total role in this situation. Help!"

SUGGESTIONS:

A. Analyze the situation:
  - Anne is not bothered by the situation so she doesn't have a problem.
  - Jack is bothered by Anne's behavior but he doesn't think the problem is his. He probably thinks it's Anne's.
  - You seem to be bothered by the whole situation. You probably have a problem with yourself in not knowing how to tactfully confront the situation. You also seem to have a problem with Anne's lack of responsibility.
  - Summary: Anne has no problem.
    Jack has a (potential one-way) problem.
    You have two (one-way) problems.

B. Apply Steps in Section: HOW THIS TOOL WORKS, page 115.

C. Be clear about your role. You will be wearing *two hats*. You will be involved in resolving your own problem while acting as a helper in facilitating Jack and Anne's problematic situation.

D. Do not be surprised if Anne "walks away" from this situation with no problem. Until she owns it, she doesn't have it. She may hear that her behavior is problem-causing to Jack and you but she doesn't have to see it as problematic for herself. Instead, she may perceive herself as helping both of you with your problems. It's her choice! Yours, too!

NOTE: MANY PEOPLE HAVE DIFFICULTY IN TALKING ABOUT OR WRITING OUT THEIR PROBLEMS. SOME PEOPLE HAVE A TENDENCY TO AVOID, IGNORE OR REJECT THEIR PROBLEMS BECAUSE THEY DO NOT KNOW HOW TO COPE WITH THEM. THE ABILITY TO RECOGNIZE AND DEFINE AN ACTUAL PROBLEM IS THE FIRST STEP IN LEARNING HOW TO MANAGE OR RESOLVE PROBLEMS. THE REST OF THE STEPS FLOW NATURALLY INTO PROBLEM MANAGEMENT OR PROBLEM RESOLUTION. THIS IS A **TRADE SECRET**.

TOOL 18

NAME CALLING

DEFINITION:

A TOOL WHICH HELPS A PERSON INITIATE AND DEVELOP A POSITIVE INTERACTION WITH ANOTHER PERSON OR GROUP BY FINDING OUT WHAT THEIR NAMES ARE, AND APPROPRIATELY USING THEIR NAMES WHEN TALKING WITH THEM. USERS WILL ALSO LEARN A METHOD FOR REMEMBERING NAMES.

HOW THIS TOOL WORKS:

1. Ask the person his or her name.
   "What is your name?"

2. Clarify a name preference when necessary.
   "Which name do you prefer, 'Robert or Bob?'"

3. Listen and give full attention to hearing the name.

   TO GIVE FULL ATTENTION:
   a. Focus your eyes on the person's face.
   b. Clear your mind of other thoughts.
   c. Do not verbally respond to any question or comment. Simply concentrate on hearing the name.

4. Say the name in a verbal tone immediately.
   "Alan."

5. Repeat his name silently to yourself at least twice.
   "Alan. Alan."
   (When you do this you are actually building a memory trace of his name in your mind.)

6. **Option Step:** Sometimes you may need to spell the person's name or ask the person to spell it for you. *"Is your name spelled A-l-a-n or A-l-l-e-n?"* (This process helps you *see* a name visually. Whenever you use this Step, remember to repeat Steps #2-4.)

7. Use the person's name a few times during the conversation or meeting. Each time you use it, you strengthen the memory trace of that name in your mind.

8. If you forget or don't remember the person's name, simply ask the person this question: *"Help me out. I forgot your name, what is it?"* (Most persons are not embarrassed to answer this question honestly.) The difficult part of this Step remains with you! The difficulty: getting you to ask *this question when you need to!*

SITUATIONS:
- During social and business introductions.
- Carrying on conversations at informal and formal events.
- Talking on the phone.
- Greeting people in offices, cafeterias, parking lots and stores.
- Directing questions and comments to specific persons at meetings.
- Recognizing the presence or absence of group members at the start-up of a meeting. (See LEGITIMIZING A MEMBER'S PRESENCE OR ABSENCE AT MEETINGS TOOL, page 109.)

BENEFITS AND PAYOFFS:
1. Gives recognition to the persons that you are talking to while treating them as people rather than as things.

2. Makes other persons feel comfortable knowing that you remember who they are.

3. Shows a caring attitude on your part and builds positive morale.

4. Gives value and status power to the person using the name and to the person being called by his or her name. Remember, names confer honor and respect!

5. Gets a person's attention. Repeated use in conversation usually results in getting the person's *undivided* or *full attention*.

6. Puts power of direction toward the person you intend to send the message to and it eliminates the need for repeating that message.

   Example: *"John, what's your idea on this project?"*

   vs.

   "What's your idea on this project?"

   (No name = no power of direction.)

EXAMPLES OF PEOPLE USING THIS TOOL:

SOCIAL SETTING: Meeting a Neighbor

(While attending a neighborhood get-together, Judy meets a new couple. During the introduction Judy hears the woman's name as "Gail.")

Judy: *"Gail. Is that spelled G-a-i-l or G-a-y-l-e?"*

Neighbor: *"G-a-y-l-e."*

Judy: *"Gayle."*

(Then she says it twice to herself while focusing her full attention on Gayle's face. As they continue to talk, Judy tactfully mentions Gayle's name about three more times.)

*   *   *

BUSINESS SETTING: Office Presentation

(A presentation is about to take place in the supervisor's office. Although everyone seems familiar to one another, Paul forgets the name of one member.)

Paul: *"I need to hear your name again. What is it?"*

Member: *"Deborah, I met you last week in Joe's office, remember?"*

Paul: *"Deborah."*

(While looking at her, he silently repeats her name twice to himself. It takes 10-12 seconds for this tool to work. At a meeting break, Paul shares some comments with Deborah and he uses her name at least twice during their conversation. By the way, Deborah is impressed with Paul's interpersonal skills and thinks highly of him.)

* * *

BUSINESS SETTING: Correspondence

(Writing an in-house memo, Pete starts off his task assignment.)

Harry,

I need a status report on this quarter's budget figures by 3:00 today. I'd appreciate your input, Harry.

Thanks,
Pete

(Notice that Pete uses Harry's name twice in his memo.)

CAUTION:

DON'T overuse the other person's name! You and I both know enough people who feel manipulated when some people use their name repeatedly in a given situation.

Reason: Most people do not want to become victims of communication games. So, don't tag every statement you make with the person's name.

DO use their name initially and then, about three more times, depending on the situation. Most people like to hear their own name! They respond more quickly when they are called by their name. They have an investment in your question because you directed it to them.

TROUBLESHOOTING:

"I'm using this tool and it doesn't seem to work for me."

NATURE OF DIFFICULTY — Problem

"During our staff meeting, I have a habit of calling on my staff members by simply addressing them as, 'Yes?' How do I break this habit? So far, I'm not having any luck."

SUGGESTIONS:

A. Be aware that half of your problem is already solved because you recognize your weakness.

B. While in the *change process*, simply add the potential speaker's name to your *"Yes?"*

Example: *"Yes, Tom?"*

Eventually, drop the word *"Yes."*

Example: *"Tom?"*

At this point you will have to train yourself to call on people by their name and they will appreciate your new behavior.

C. List your benefits for addressing people by their name. Remember, when people hear their name, they listen more acutely to the message.

NATURE OF DIFFICULTY — Problem

"During most introductions I get distracted and I don't catch the name of the new person. Then, I'm too embarrassed to ask the person his or her name. What do you suggest?"

SUGGESTIONS:

A. Give *full* attention to the introduction. Since our minds can program about 500 words per minute, your mind is obviously programming other ideas during this time. Prepare yourself for each introduction by clearing your mind of all ideas and focus on the person's name.

B. Admit your problem by saying:

"Help me out. What is your name? I got distracted."

C. Do the Steps listed in this Tool under the heading HOW THIS TOOL WORKS on page 121.

NOTE: THERE IS GREAT POWER IN A NAME. MOST PEOPLE ARE NOT AWARE OF THIS FACT. THEREFORE, LISTEN TO A PERSON'S NAME. WHEN YOU HEAR THE NAME, SAY IT ALOUD IMMEDIATELY. DEVELOP EXPERTISE IN THE USE OF THIS TOOL. YOU'LL SOON REALIZE WHY THIS TOOL IS A **TRADE SECRET**.

TOOL 19

PARAPHRASING OR RESTATING

DEFINITION:

A TOOL FOR CHECKING COMMUNICATION ACCURACY BETWEEN SPEAKERS AND LISTENERS. PARAPHRASING IS SAYING BACK TO THE SPEAKER, *IN YOUR OWN WORDS*, YOUR UNDERSTANDING OF WHAT THE SPEAKER HAS JUST SAID. EITHER SPEAKERS OR LISTENERS MAY USE THIS TOOL.

HOW THIS TOOL WORKS:

1. Listen to the speaker's *intended* message.

2. Ask for clarification of specific words when necessary.
   "Jo, what does 'ameliorate' mean?"

3. Begin to restate by using the *speaker's name* and *a stem phrase*, which *clues* the speaker in that you are going to paraphrase his or her message.

   HERE'S HOW TO DO THIS:
   "Jo, are you saying . . ."
   "Tom, you're saying that . . ."
   "Judy, let me see if I'm hearing you correctly."
   "Marilyn, what I'm getting from you is . . ."

4. Continue your paraphrasing and *key* into the speaker's major points. Put emphasis on the same points as the speaker does.

5. Finish your paraphrasing and allow the speaker to accept or reject your restatement.

If the speaker doesn't accept your restatement, ask the speaker *to repeat* the part that you incorrectly restated. Then, paraphrase *that part* of the statement to the speaker's satisfaction.

An Example

Pete: *"Bill, you're saying that all the vans need oil checks, right?"*

Bill: *"Not exactly, Pete. I'm saying that the condition of the green vans causes me to wonder about your maintenance system for all our vans."*

(Bill doesn't accept Pete's restatement.)

Pete: *"Okay, Bill. I think I have it now. Because of the oil leak in the green vans, you're concerned about how I keep check on the general condition of all the vans."*

Bill: *"You got it."*

(Bill accepts Pete's restatement.)

6. Avoid repeating the exact words of the speaker and at no time inject your own opinion into your restatement.

   (*See above example.* Pete tried to inject his opinion into Bill's statement. Bill rejected Pete's first restatement.)

7. Have the courage to say "No" to a paraphrase that is not correct. Otherwise, you may pay a price later for allowing misunderstandings to develop in your conversations.

8. **Option Step:** If you, as a speaker, wish to initiate a paraphrase from your listener, simply ask one of the following questions:

   — *"Pete, what message are you getting so far?"*

   — *"Pete, I'm not sure I'm giving you a clear message. What are you hearing?"*

   — *"Pete, what is your understanding of the assignment?"*

9. Work to achieve mutual understanding, either as a listener or speaker.

SITUATIONS:

- Receiving an assignment or a job and wanting to achieve understanding at the time you receive it.
- Getting clarification on a complex issue.
- Summarizing another person's point of view.
- Receiving a telephone number or address while talking on the phone.
- Buying an item and then checking with the clerk to verify that what you *think* you purchased is *exactly* what you purchased.
- Debating an issue with another person and making certain that you heard all points correctly before you take the *defensive* or *offensive position*.
- Sending a message to the speaker that you *got-the-point*. Paraphrasing *usually stops* the speaker from repeating his or her message to you.

BENEFITS AND PAYOFFS:

1. Ensures an adequate level of understanding between the speaker and the listener.

2. Eliminates *rumor growth*! Messages are checked immediately.

3. Gives the other person an opportunity to think about what she or he has just said.

4. Stimulates the speaker to clarify necessary points that may typically be assumed because of the speaker's familiarity with the item or subject.

5. Recognizes the other person's input as *worthy of being heard and understood*.

6. Creates a climate for dialogue and maintains an adult-to-adult relationship.

7. Boosts morale by having someone *take time* to listen to another's ideas and actually *hear* what is being said.

8. Saves time which is lost through misunderstandings.

9. Increases a person's feelings of success in acquiring better listening skills.

EXAMPLES OF PEOPLE USING THIS TOOL:

SOCIAL SETTING
(Listener initiates the paraphrase.)

Chris: *"How does it sound, dad?"*

Dad: *"Chris, let's see if I'm understanding your idea. You're going to put in 50% of the money and you want me to put in the other 50%. Is that it?"*

Chris: *"Sounds like you got my message, dad."*

    (Chris is satisfied with what he hears.)

*   *   *

BUSINESS SETTING
(Speaker initiates the paraphrase.)

Speaker: *"Pat, I think organizational climate affects motivation, absenteeism and turnover of employees. What are you getting from my comment, Pat?"*

Pat: *"You feel that an organization can be influenced by motivational factors, employee turnovers and the number of absentees. Right?"*

Speaker: *"Well, yeah, and I also think . . ."*

    (Speaker is satisfied and wants to continue.)

CAUTION:

DON'T psychoanalyze why the speaker feels or thinks the way he or she does. And, don't go beyond the original meaning of the speaker. If you do, you are not using this tool properly.

Reason: Some people, under the guise of paraphrasing, use probing and interview tools while believing they are simply restating another person's opinions. When you paraphrase, you do not share *your opinion* on the speaker's subject — nor do you ask questions relating to *why* the speaker holds such opinions.

DO plan to use questions and other discussion tools to build mutual understanding among people. Just be clear which tool you are using and why you are using the tool. A timely and correct use of paraphrasing in a discussion will deepen the level of understanding between people.

TROUBLESHOOTING:

"I'm using this tool and it doesn't seem to work for me."

NATURE OF DIFFICULTY — Problem

"As Vice President of Sales I've been observing one of my regional managers handling questions from his staff. I'm aware that he does not answer their questions succinctly, directly or logically. Since I'm not one of his staff members, what's the best way for me to help him? I know his listening skills are poor!"

SUGGESTIONS:

A. Give the regional manager some feedback at the break or at the close of one of his staff meetings.

— If he is familiar with this Tool, ask him to restate each question of the staff member before he responds to it.

— Tell the manager that his restatement must be accepted by the staff member *before* he can begin to answer the staff member's question.

— Suggest that he end his answer with a direct question to his staff member.

An Example

"Have I addressed your question adequately, Mary?"

B. Use Video Tape for training in this Tool. Record actual Sales Meetings and Training Sessions. Model the use of these Tools.

NOTE: IF YOU ARE BEING PARAPHRASED, YOU NEED TO BE WILLING TO SAY *"YES"* WHEN THE PARAPHRASE IS ACCURATE. YOU NEED TO BE WILLING TO SAY *"NO"* WHEN THE PARAPHRASE IS NOT ACCURATE. YOU MUST CORRECT MISUNDERSTANDINGS AND KEEP THE FOCUS ON YOUR ORIGINAL IDEA. IF YOU DO THE ABOVE, YOU WILL BE USING A **TRADE SECRET.**

TOOL 20
POSITIVE DISCIPLINING

DEFINITION:

A TOOL WHICH GIVES THE *PERSON-IN-CHARGE* A PROACTIVE PROCEDURE FOR IMPROVING A PERSON'S WORK PERFORMANCE. USERS OF THIS TOOL FOCUS THEIR ENERGIES ON MODIFYING UNDESIRABLE BEHAVIORS AND REWARDING DESIRABLE BEHAVIORS WITH CERTAIN PEOPLE.

HOW THIS TOOL WORKS:

1. Determine what is causing an employee's work performance to be unacceptable to you.

   "The employee lacks follow-through skills. Several tasks are incomplete even though I give him reminders on each incomplete area."

2. Ask for the employee's cooperation in resolving *your problem* with his work performance.

   "I need your cooperation, Ted. I'm having a problem with, what I perceive to be, your lack of follow-through skills. Will you help me resolve my problem?"

3. Describe, by sharing details and other pertinent data, your reasons for finding his behavior unacceptable.

   HERE'S HOW TO DO IT:

   a. Provide actual cases of incomplete tasks and their effects on the organization.

   b. Cite dates, memos, ticklers, and other documented conversations.

    c. Discuss these *findings* with the employee.

    d. Keep an active listening posture (see ACTIVE LISTENING TOOL, page 1). Use restatement, when necessary, and send *"I-messages"* when possible. (See PROBLEM OWNERSHIP TOOL: Caution Section, page 145.)

4. Ask for and initiate appropriate steps to modify the employee's current work behavior.

FIRST STEP: GET THE EMPLOYEE'S IDEAS.

> *"I would appreciate your suggestions for improving your follow-through skills."*

(Wait for suggestions to surface. Write down mutually acceptable ones.)

SECOND STEP: GIVE YOUR IDEAS.

> *"I have some suggestions, too. Please realize the need I have for solid follow-through skills with the type of work both of us do."*

(Ask the employee to write down mutually acceptable ones.)

5. Decide, by consensus, which behavior will be practiced. Both parties need to document the decision with signatures. Include in the written statement:

    a. New behavior.

    b. Dates of review and monitor sessions.

    c. Results or rewards for doing or not doing the behavior.

6. Provide informal, positive feedback frequently.

HERE'S AN EXAMPLE:

"Ted, I want to commend you for meeting the deadline this morning. The work looks great. Keep it up."

(See CREDITING TOOL, page 45.)

Cautiously, give constructive, negative feedback as needed.
(See GIVING FEEDBACK TOOL, page 87.)

SITUATIONS:

- Clarifying job responsibilities.
- Clarifying levels of authority on delegated tasks.
- Reviewing progress or lack of progress.
- Instructing a trainee.
- Confronting a difficult employee.
- Administering positive discipline in a proactive manner.
- Coaching or counseling an employee.
- Acting as a change agent for someone who is having a problem.
- Dealing with poor attendance, misconduct or performance problems.
- Negotiating for different (more acceptable) behaviors.

BENEFITS AND PAYOFFS:

1. Resolves problems at an early stage rather than using avoidance techniques.

2. Equips the user with a procedure for tackling difficult employees.

3. Provides the user with an adult-to-adult method for giving constructive feedback in a professional manner.

4. Protects the administrator. There is a tactful way to give constructive, negative feedback to an employee.

5. Overcomes the distaste some persons have for not wanting to deal directly with work problems involving their employees.

6. Generates an increase in positive morale among users when they know how to cope with difficult employee-employer situations.

7. Enables a user to handle appraisal sessions with ease.

8. Develops self accountability by targeting problem behaviors and approaches to use to resolve those problems. (This Tool involves both parties in Problem Resolution.)

9. Kills *scapegoating* by starving the *scapegoat*. This means that someone identifies, owns, and systematically deals with the problem.

EXAMPLES OF PEOPLE USING THIS TOOL:

BUSINESS SETTING

The case:

(Matt, a supervisor, finds Sid's work performance unacceptable. The following script indicates some of the steps Matt takes to deal with his problem.)

(Talking to himself.)

Step 1.　I need to determine Sid's precise work behavior that is causing me a problem. Sid is supposed to process 10 forms per hour. He currently processes 5-7 forms per hour. *I'm having a problem with his rate production.*

(Talking to himself.)

Step 2.　I'll arrange a meeting with Sid to ask his cooperation in resolving my problem.

(Talking to Sid.)
"Sid, I need to arrange a meeting with you. I'm having a problem with your production rate these past two days. I feel certain you can help me. What about 2:00 p.m. for about 25 minutes? 2:00-2:25 p.m. Okay?"

(Talking to himself.)
When the meeting begins, I say:

(Talking to Sid)
"Sid, I know you are capable of completing 10 forms per hour. Lately, you've been completing 5-7 forms per hour. Help me understand what is happening."

(Talking to himself.)
At no time do I blame him or use aggressive behavior.

(Talking to himself.)
Step 3. I listen to Sid's view. I maintain good eye contact.

Now, I need to tell him my view.

(Talking to Sid.)
"Sid, I understand your view of the slow-down in production. I'd like to share with you the effect the reduced rate is having on my volume of servicing customer complaints."

(Talking to himself.)
When each of us has been heard, I ask for his suggestions for resolving my problem.

(Talking to himself.)
Step 4. I follow the rest of the Steps as outlined in the Section: HOW THIS TOOL WORKS, page 133.

CAUTION:

DON'T fail to realize that in the use of this tool, you will usually meet with some degree of resistance from the person whose work performance you find unacceptable. Be ready to overcome this resistance!

Reason: As humans, we want to do what is right and when our actions fall short of this goal, we normally have a hard time getting *back on track*. Most of us do not like others pointing out our shortcomings. Most of us resist someone giving us advice as to how we could improve ourselves. We show our resistance by using blame behaviors. We blame others; we blame machines; we blame our working conditions. Rarely do we accept ourselves as the source of the blame or problem.

DO learn to overcome resistance by actively listening to the complaints and blame statements of the other. Then, seek ways to *empower* the other person by focusing on their positive points. To empower the person means *to give a person the assurance that you believe in their ability to take responsibility, and you value their contribution when it measures up to your standards of acceptability.*

TROUBLESHOOTING:

"I'm using this tool and it doesn't seem to work for me."

NATURE OF DIFFICULTY — Problem

"I'm having a problem with my receptionist. She has poor communication skills. She's causing me problems, and my patients are reacting in a negative manner toward her. I've asked her for suggestions on how we could improve the situation and she gives me *no ideas!* What should I do?"

SUGGESTIONS:

A. Consider the way you are asking her for suggestions. Hopefully, you are asking open-ended questions. (See OPEN-ENDED QUESTIONS TOOL, page 9.)

B. Continue to probe for a positive commitment from the person to modify her behavior. Together, seek to find payoffs that will motivate the person to want to improve her behavior. (See USING MOTIVATORS AND PAYOFFS TOOL, page 165, for help in motivation techniques.)

C. Commit yourself to study the situation thoroughly. Tell the person you will do this. However, state your need for the person to modify her behavior. At *times,* you will need to put "all your cards on the table." At *all times*, stay in your adult behavior. Do not allow yourself to *slip* into a parent mode. Send "I-messages" and stay in your adult mode. Good luck!

NOTE: THE SUCCESS OR FAILURE OF USING THIS TOOL RESTS MAINLY WITH YOU! ESSENTIAL ELEMENTS IN MAKING THIS TOOL WORK PROPERLY ARE: YOUR ATTITUDE, YOUR KNOWLEDGE OF THE PERSON'S JOB, YOUR AWARENESS OF THE PERSON'S SKILL IN DOING THE JOB AND YOUR UNDERSTANDING OF HOW THIS TOOL WORKS. REMEMBER, FOCUS YOUR ATTENTION ON THE BEHAVIOR NEEDING IMPROVEMENT RATHER THAN FOCUSING YOUR ATTENTION ON CHANGING THE PERSONALITY OF THE WORKER. WHEN YOU USE THIS TOOL, YOU ARE USING A **TRADE SECRET**!

TOOL 21

PROBLEM OWNERSHIP

DEFINITION:

A TOOL FOR HELPING PEOPLE RECOGNIZE PROBLEMS, DETERMINE THEIR CAUSES, AND IDENTIFY THEIR OWNERS TO GET CORRECT DEFINITIONS OF THOSE PROBLEMS. USERS OF THIS TOOL LEARN A PROCEDURE FOR FORMULATING PROPER PROBLEM STATEMENTS.

HOW THIS TOOL WORKS:

1. Analyze the current situation. Ask yourself this question:

   "Does a problem exist?"

2. Consider these points:
   a. Problems exist when peoples' needs are not being met.
   b. There is no problem when each person's needs are being met satisfactorily.
   c. A problem must be owned by someone for a situation to be problematic.

3. Decide whether a problem exists or does not exist.

4. Determine the nature of the problem.

   People usually have problems when they find certain behaviors unacceptable in themselves or other people.

5. Determine who owns the problem. Ask youself the question:

   "Who owns the problem? Who seems bothered by the current situation?"

6. Decide if the problem is one-way or two-way in terms of its ownership.

   a. A one-way problem is owned by *one* person. The other person does not have to own the problem too.

   b. *One-way problem owners* usually *assume* the other person is also having the same problem. This is a false assumption!

   c. A *two-way problem* is the same problem owned by both parties. This is a rarity!

7. Use verbal expressions which imply someone's ownership of the problem.

   One-way expressions: *"My problem is . . ."*
   "I have a problem . . ."

   Two-way expressions: *"We have a problem."*
   "Our problem is . . ."

8. Proceed to manage your problem or act as a helper to someone who needs to solve a problem. (See MANAGING AND RESOLVING PROBLEMS TOOL, page 115.)

9. **Remember:** A person has a problem only when he or she owns it. If there is no owner, there is no problem. You'll need to call the situation something other than a problem.

10. **Option Step:** You may want to use the *Problem Identification Form* on page 148.

SITUATIONS:
- Identifying a problem and its owner.
- Locating the source of confusion.
- Analyzing sources of potential trouble.
- Managing personal stress from a holistic position.
- Managing a family argument using a cause and effect approach.

- Eliminating unwanted personal behavior patterns.
- Acting as a change agent for a person or group by helping involved parties *iron out* their differences.

BENEFITS AND PAYOFFS:

1. Reduces levels of stress which result from ineffective management of problems.

2. Confronts potential problems using proactive tools.

3. Helps you realize other solutions to problems once you have determined who owns the problem.

4. Enables you to approach problems systematically.

5. Focuses the *blame* for an existing problem on a person or persons who choose to own such *blame*.

6. Teaches you how to help people identify their problems and other peoples' problems.

7. Allows you to function, as a change agent, for other people involved in problems affecting their work.

8. Saves you money by helping you identify problems at their "front-end."

EXAMPLES OF PEOPLE USING THIS TOOL:

SOCIAL SETTING

(A teenager is mad at his parents for locking him out of the house. He had been visiting friends next door and his parents assumed he had his key with him.)

Friend: *"Paul, obviously you're angry with your parents. But whose problem is it?"*

(Friend is analyzing the problem and trying to identify the owner.)

Paul: *"It's their fault. They should know I don't carry my key around with me all day.*

(Fault = problem in Paul's opinion. Paul believes it's his parents' problem.)

Friend: *"Paul, I don't think they meant to lock you out. Besides, they're not bothered by the situation — they don't even know about it — so, it can't be their problem or fault."*

(Friend helps Paul to clarify his thinking.)

Paul: *"Well, you've got a point. If I'm the only one angry, then I guess it's my problem. Anyway, I'm mad!"*

(Paul owns the problem. At this point it is a one-way problem.)

* * *

BUSINESS SETTING

(Customers are receiving nasty responses from the clerk when they call for service repair. The service technicians are receiving these complaints from their customers. Working conditions are bad! The office manager confronts his clerk with the situation. The clerk says she is too busy to do anything right.)

Manager: *"So, you're saying you have a problem with your workload, and this causes you to answer the phones abruptly?"*

(The manager actively listens to analyze the problem.)

Clerk: *"Exactly. I admit I've been a bit snappy to some of the customers. I'd like to blame them or my work or something. I'm just not able to cope with all these pressures. I'm glad you've taken the time to hear me out."*

(The clerk admits her problem. At this point it's one-way.)

Manager: *"Well, I was having a problem with deciding how to talk to you about this situation. Now I feel we can work out something to better the situation. How about . . ."*

(Manager admits his problem *which is not the same as his clerk's.* His problem is one-way.)

* * *

AVOID THE FOLLOWING EXPRESSIONS:

"The problem is . . ."

(In this expression there is no ownership. If there is a problem, someone has to own it.)

"Our problem is . . ."

(This expression implies two-way ownership and both parties may not be owning the problem.)

CAUTION:

DON'T send or use "You-messages" when talking about problems. For example: *"You have a problem and you should get on it immediately."*

Reason: "You-messages" are indicative of GOD-talk; these are messages that are authoritative and absolute. Such messages leave *no room* for responders to realistically defend their actions. As a result of receiving a "You-message," a responder often feels rebellious, resentful and threatened.

DO send or use "I-messages" when talking about your problems. "I-messages" are honest expressions of people who own their feelings and are responsible for their behaviors. For example, *"I'm having a problem with your coming home late and I'm upset with your behavior. I want you to know how I'm feeling."*

At times it's risky business to send "I-messages," because you leave yourself open and vulnerable to other people who may think that owning problems is a sign of weakness. However, you choose how you want to handle their perceptions.

TROUBLESHOOTING:

"I'm using this tool and it doesn't seem to work for me."

NATURE OF DIFFICULTY

"I am a supervisor. I'm having a problem with Bill, my team leader. He uses vulgar language and some of his team members are becoming very upset with him. They have asked me to speak to him about his problem. Now, I don't think he has a problem! I think his employees do! So how do I confront them with their problem when they don't think they have one?"

SUGGESTIONS:

A. Use the *Problem Identification Form*. (See *Form*, page 148.)

Ask each of them to fill out the *Form*. Then, have a discussion with them. Focus on the sixth statement of the *Form*.

B. Review the Steps of this Tool, page 141. Stress the points relating to one-way and two-way problems. Help the employees to see that they may be having a one-way problem with Bill.

C. Talk to Bill. He may be unaware of the effects his language is having on his coworkers. Bill may want to change his behavior because of the negative payoffs he receives when he hears how his coworkers feel toward him. (See USING MOTIVATORS AND PAYOFFS TOOL, page 165.)

NOTE: A PROBLEM PROPERLY IDENTIFIED AND OWNED IS A PROBLEM HALF SOLVED! MANY PEOPLE WASTE TIME ATTEMPTING TO SOLVE UNIDENTIFIED OR NON-OWNED PROBLEMS. FORMULATING A PROPER PROBLEM STATE-MENT IS SOMETIMES MORE IMPORTANT THAN ITS SOLUTION. THIS IS A **TRADE SECRET**!

PROBLEM IDENTIFICATION FORM

Complete each step before proceeding to the next step.

1. Write down *the problem* which seems most important to you at this time.

2. Does your problem statement include *who* is hurting or feeling the pinch? If not, rewrite your problem statement to include the person or persons.

3. Does your problem statement include *your involvement* with the problem? How you are feeling? How the problem is affecting you? If not, rewrite your problem statement to include your involvement.

4. Write down *who* or *what* is causing the problem. Examples: others, subgroup, total group, parent, boss. Avoid the response, "Everyone is causing the problem." Be specific. Which group or what condition is causing the problem?

5. Write down the *kind of problem* it is. Examples: communication, time, conflict of values, inability to tolerate certain kinds of behavior, lack of skill, inadequate resources. Be specific.

6. Now, write *your problem* again! Include all the elements listed above.

TOOL 22

TIME CONTRACTING

DEFINITION:

A TOOL FOR HELPING PEOPLE WHO CHAIR OR ATTEND MEETINGS TO MANAGE THEIR TIME PRODUCTIVELY. USERS OF THIS TOOL APPLY *START-UP* AND *END-TIMES* TO THEIR MEETINGS.

HOW THIS TOOL WORKS:

CHAIRPERSONS

1. Give the starting time of your meeting.

   "The meeting will be held in the Conference Room at 9:00 a.m."

2. Give the ending time of your meeting.

   "Meeting time: 9:00-9:45 a.m."

   Give precise time frames.

3. Negotiate if more time is needed.

   HERE'S HOW:

   a. Five minutes before the scheduled ending time, ask the person or group members for more time.

   b. Be precise about the amount of additional time.
      "I need fifteen more minutes."

   c. Actually negotiate for more time by addressing members by name.

      You: *"I need to extend our end-time by fifteen minutes. How about your schedule, Tom? Any problem?"*

Tom: *"No problem."*

You: *"What about you, Jan?"*
(Wait for her response.)

Jan: *"It's okay with me."*

You: *"Fine, let's continue. Our new end-time will be 10:00 a.m."*

d. If some members are not able to extend their time at this meeting, reschedule the group for another time. Negotiation involves many options.

e. If most members are able to stay, negotiate for departing members to receive briefing. This can be arranged between members.

"Ted and John, since you have to leave, check with someone here to brief you on these last two items, okay?"

ATTENDEES

1. State the amount of time you'll need when making appointments.

"I'll need twenty minutes."

Due to the nature of some appointments, you may not know how much time you'll need. In such cases, ask the secretary for the time frame.

You: *"How much time will it take?"*

Secretary: *"About an hour."*

You: *"Fine, I'll be there at 3:30 till 4:30 p.m. Thank you."*

2. Ask for the ending time of a meeting.

HERE'S HOW:

a. You receive a meeting announcement. There is a starting time but no end-time. You make a phone call to the chairperson or to his or her secretary and say, *"I need to know what time the meeting will end. Please let me know by noon today. Thank you."*

b. **Option:** A meeting is about to start and you do not know the ending time. You ask, *"What time will this meeting end?"*

3. Be aware of your right to know time frames which involve your presence with other people. Choose to use or not to use this right.

SITUATIONS:

- Planning and announcing your meetings. (All types.)
- Chairing a meeting.
- Chairing a meeting that runs overtime due to poor time-management practices.
- Scheduling appointments with a receptionist or secretary.
- Attending meetings that do not specify ending times.
- Organizing your day's work. It's important to *time contract with yourself*! Learn to use your own time well! Actually schedule appointments with yourself. Example: 11:00-12:00 (My time — Review Project B).
- Managing certain types of meetings. As chairperson, you have not stated an end-time. On these occasions, you say, *"I have not placed an end-time on this meeting due to the nature of our business today."*

BENEFITS AND PAYOFFS:

1. Demonstrates your belief that people have important things to do after your meeting.

2. Helps you share your power by telling people what time your meeting will end. Information is power. When you share it, you empower your staff members to participate in a well-organized meeting. They tend to remind you of your stated end-times and they will remind you to negotiate for additional time if needed.

3. Allows people to fully participate in your meeting because they know your time frames. An *informed* participant is an *involved* participant.

4. Shows respect for the other persons. You are using *their* time and you're using it effectively.

5. Indicates to the listener that you mean what you say. Rather than saying, *"Have you a minute,"* and not meaning that, you say, *"What are you doing now, Joe? It's 9:30 a.m."*

6. Provides you with a system for prioritizing your work. Your meetings and appointments are set in time frames that contain end-times.

7. Empowers you, as an attendee, to exercise your right to know how long you will be "tied up" and unable to do your planned work.

EXAMPLES OF PEOPLE USING THIS TOOL:

SOCIAL SETTING: Dinner Invitation

(Jo invites Cindy and her husband to dinner.)

Jo: *"Hi, Cindy. If you haven't plans for this Saturday night, what about coming for dinner?"*

Cindy: *"Looks good. We're free and we would love to come. What time shall we be there?"*

Jo: *"Come around 7:00."*

Cindy: *"Jo, how long shall we plan to stay?"*

Jo: *"Till we all get tired! How's that?"*

Cindy: *"Well, I'd feel better if we set a time. Let's say we'll stay till 11:00 p.m., okay?"*

(Cindy sets an end-time. So, when the time comes, she will simply and comfortably leave.)

Jo: *"Sounds great!"*

* * *

BUSINESS SETTING: Staff Meeting

Memo: There will be a staff meeting on Monday from 1:00-2:15 p.m.

(Notice the ending time!)

BUSINESS SETTING: Appointment

Division Head: *"I'd like to make an appointment with Mrs. Allen. I'll need about 25 minutes. When would be a good time for her to meet with me?"*

Secretary: *"Eleven o'clock this morning."*

Division Head: *"Fine. I'll meet with her from 11:00 till 11:25 a.m. Thanks."*

* * *

BUSINESS SETTING: Appointment

Office Manager: *"I'll need about 10 minutes of your time. Will 9:30 to 9:40 a.m. be okay with you, Alice?"*

Dental Hygienist: *"Yes, Barb. I'll be able to meet with you then. I don't have another patient till 10:00 a.m."*

CAUTION:

DON'T develop habits of stating time in approximate time frames. Here are some typical expressions:
1. *"Have you a minute?"*
2. *"It may take the whole afternoon to finish that project."*
3. *"Can you hold for a second?"*

Reason: Our language can be extremely deceptive. When we say, *"Can we meet for about 15 minutes,"* we may mean 20-25 minutes while the listener may mean 15 minutes exactly.

DO develop habits of stating time in precise terms. If necessary, negotiate for more time. However, work to end at your stated time. A basic rule of good communication is: *Never over estimate the amount of knowledge the receiver possesses.*

TROUBLESHOOTING:

"I'm using this tool and it doesn't seem to work for me."

NATURE OF DIFFICULTY — Problem

"My director gives the end-times for his meetings. However, he doesn't honor them and he doesn't negotiate for additional time. We just sit there like *clock watchers*. How can someone set an end-time and deliberately violate its meaning? What are we supposed to do?"

SUGGESTIONS:

A. Take a proactive role in this situation. Ask the director if one of you can monitor the ending time of his meetings.

   HERE'S HOW:

   Five minutes before the scheduled end-time, a person signals the director, either nonverbally or verbally, to remind him of the time.

B. Review the Step on Negotiations and use it. (See Chairpersons, Step #3, page 149.)

C. Practice some assertive behaviors with your director. (See BEING ASSERTIVE TOOL, page 15.)

NATURE OF DIFFICULTY — Problem

"My boss called and said she'd like to see me this afternoon when I'm free. How do I tell her that I have only 15 minutes to spare today? Also, she forgot to tell me how long she plans to keep me and I'm not certain she knows about giving end-times. Help me out."

SUGGESTIONS:

A. Call her secretary back and ask her to check the length of your meeting. Inform the secretary that you're on a tight schedule today and can only stay for 15 minutes. Ask her to give you a call back with this information.

B. **Option:** Appear at the meeting and tactfully inform your boss of your 15 minute time frame. If necessary, be willing to renegotiate for another day and time. Remember, it's your right to know time frames. Although it's risk-taking behavior to ask for time frames, you're being proactive and most bosses will respect you for "speaking up."

NOTE: EVERY MEETING THAT'S EVER BEEN HELD HAS ENDED! EVERY MEETING THAT'S EVER BEEN HELD HAS HAD AN END-TIME, TOO! SO, WHY NOT STATE YOUR END-TIMES ON YOUR MEMOS OR AT THE BEGINNING OF YOUR MEETINGS? THEN, YOU'LL ALWAYS BE RUNNING YOUR MEETINGS INSTEAD OF YOUR MEETINGS RUNNING YOU. THIS IS A **TRADE SECRET**.

TOOL 23

UNDERSTANDING AGREEMENT OR DISAGREEMENT

DEFINITION:

A TOOL WHICH BUILDS MUTUAL UNDERSTANDING AMONG PEOPLE WITHOUT NEEDING OR ASKING THEM TO AGREE WITH THE IDEA, STATEMENT OR DECISION. ALTHOUGH SOME SPEAKERS WILL WANT THEIR LISTENERS TO AGREE WITH THEM, AGREEMENT IS NOT ESSENTIAL TO THE UNDERSTANDING PROCESS.

HOW THIS TOOL WORKS:

1. Keep an open mind by *clearing your mind* of your thoughts on the subject you're listening to.

2. Listen to understand by taking on a *nonevaluative posture*. Try to understand the person from that person's point of view. Don't become defensive or judgmental when you hear the other's idea; rather, see the idea from the speaker's frame of reference.

   HERE'S HOW TO DO THIS:

   a. Ask clarifying questions, when necessary.

   b. Restate or paraphrase what you are hearing.

   c. Sense how it feels to the speaker.

   d. *Walk around in his or her shoes* for a while.

   e. Use a "test case" to check your ability to understand the speaker's emphasis, attitude and major points.

3. Say, "*I understand*" when you honestly do!

REMINDER

Most listeners *assume* their speakers know when understanding has occurred.

Most speakers *assume* they are not understood until their listeners make some type of verbal response.

4. Avoid adding agreement or disagreement statements to your response when these statements are not required in the understanding process.

Remember: To agree or disagree, you must first understand what is being said to you.

5. **Option Step:** If you decide to add an agreement or disagreement statement to your response, here are some statements to use:
   a. *"I understand and agree."*
   b. *"I understand and partially agree."*
   c. *"I understand and want you to know I disagree with your third reason . . ."* (Be specific in terms of *what* you disagree with. Allow the other person to ask *why* you disagree. Sometimes, the other person isn't interested in knowing why.)

6. Know that *commitment and support* are involved in the understanding phase rather than in the agreement/disagreement phase.

You can understand, be committed and support another's position or decision, without having to agree or disagree with it.

SITUATIONS:

- Delegating assignments.
- Communicating ideas to another person or a group.
- Debating different points of view.
- Conducting Briefing Sessions.
- Learning new methods and approaches.

- Giving verbal support to another's views.
- Overcoming the tendency to *"Yes, but"* people. (Instead of assuming quick understanding [*"Yes"*], followed by a disagreement [*"but"*], take more time and build a deeper degree of understanding.)
- Selling and buying situations.
- Demonstrating participatory management principles.

BENEFITS AND PAYOFFS:

1. Generates positive feelings of respect from others.

2. Produces effective and efficient delegations.

3. Develops insight into another person's frame of reference which results in mutual understanding.

4. Allows you to manage confrontations, using inter-personal skills.

5. Provides you with an opportunity to talk to others without you becoming highly emotional and defensive when others disagree with your ideas.

6. Helps you tap more creative ideas from others because they feel that you really want to listen to what they have to say.

7. Demonstrates an attitude of care which influences others to listen to you. (When a person *has been listened to*, he or she is inclined to listen to that person.)

8. Facilitates a win/win dialogue rather than a win/lose monologue.

EXAMPLES OF PEOPLE USING THIS TOOL:

SOCIAL SETTING

(Four people are playing a card game. A conflict begins when one player [Joe] interprets a rule differently from the rest.)

Joe: *"I've been listening to what the three of you have been saying. I understand how you see it."*

(He lets them know he has kept an open mind and he is able to understand them. He does not tell them he disagrees with them.)

Al: *"Do you agree with us?"*

Joe: *"I disagree with the way you've interpreted the third point. However, I can live with your meaning and we can continue to play."*

(Now, Joe tells them where he disagrees with them and he also tells them that he can support their interpretation. He's in a win/win frame of mind.)

* * *

BUSINESS SETTING

(A Real Estate agent and a client are in a discussion regarding the terms of a contract.)

Agent: *"Your second bid proposal was finally accepted. There is one change that I need to discuss with you. The seller wishes to move up the closing date by 15 days."*

Client: *"I understand and accept the new closing date. It doesn't present any problems for me."*

(In this example, understanding and agreement are necessary, since the entire contract is titled: REAL ESTATE PURCHASE AND SALE AGREEMENT.)

CAUTION:

DON'T use the following verbal expressions:
"Have you got that?"   *"Do you understand?"*
"Have I made myself clear?"   *"Ok?"*
"You know what I mean, don't you?"   *"Got it?"*
These expressions may lead you nowhere. So, if you use them, be careful!

Reason: Although some people may respond with a *"Yes"* answer to any one of the above questions, there is no guarantee they understand what you have said to them. Many people give an automatic *"Yes"* answer because they do not wish to appear ignorant.

Also, some people are not willing to ask questions when they don't understand. So, when you ask these people if they understand, they simply say *"Yes"* and give you a dishonest answer. No one wins in such a situation and mutual understanding does not occur.

DO develop new, verbal expressions for checking the other person's understanding. (See PARAPHRASING TOOL, Step #3, page 127.) Be slow to ask for his or her agreement, especially in situations where it is not required.

TROUBLESHOOTING:

"I'm using this tool and it doesn't seem to work for me."

NATURE OF DIFFICULTY — Problem

"My problem is with computer salespeople. I needed to know the basics of a specific computer, and this salesman began telling me everything he knew about computers. From my point of view, he was batting 'zero' until I told him I wasn't understanding much of what he was saying. I couldn't believe my ears! After I told him I didn't understand, he began giving me his *sales pitch* again. There's got to be a better way to get my message across. Any suggestions?"

SUGGESTIONS:

A. Interrupt his *sales pitch* when misunderstanding takes place.

HERE'S HOW TO DO IT:

"Dale, I do not understand that last function. I need you to go much slower, and you might be more helpful to me if I worked the keyboard and you observed me."

B. Do not allow misunderstandings to *pile up*. Stop the action by using assertive expressions.

(See BEING ASSERTIVE TOOL, page 15.)

C. Continue to use assertive expressions. When you understand the functions, tell him so!

HERE'S HOW:

"Dale, I understand the functions. Thanks for your time."

NATURE OF DIFFICULTY — Problem

"I tend to use the verbal expression, 'Any questions?' when finishing a briefing or discussion session with my staff. I realize that this is my way of saying, 'Do you understand what I've said to you?' The staff doesn't say much, so I'm not getting a good reading from them. Are there better ways to find out if they're understanding me?"

SUGGESTIONS:

A. Be more specific with your questions and address staff members by name. You will definitely get responses from them.

HERE ARE SOME EXAMPLES:

— *"Joyce, what are your comments on this recommendation to update our equipment?"*

— *"Jim, what questions do you have on the first item?"*

— *"Bill, what are you getting from my pitch regarding aircraft improvements?"*

B. Use paraphrasing to help you check for communication accuracy.

(See PARAPHRASING TOOL, page 127.)

NOTE: MANY PEOPLE EQUATE LIKING WITH AGREE-
MENT AND DISLIKING WITH DISAGREEMENT.
IN REALITY, THEY ARE NOT EQUATABLE. A
PERSON CAN UNDERSTAND AND LIKE WHAT
HE OR SHE HEARS AND NOT AGREE WITH IT.

Example: *"I understand your method of resolving
this issue — I like it too — but I disagree that it's
the method you should use at this time."*

USE THIS TOOL AND YOU'LL BE USING A
TRADE SECRET.

TOOL 24

USING MOTIVATORS AND PAYOFFS

DEFINITION:

A TOOL FOR GETTING PEOPLE TO IDENTIFY REASONS WHY THEY ARE THE WAY THEY ARE AND WHY THEY ACT THE WAY THEY DO. ONCE PEOPLE UNDERSTAND THESE REASONS OR PAYOFFS, THEY CAN CHOOSE TO IMPROVE, CHANGE OR REMAIN THE SAME.

HOW THIS TOOL WORKS:

Please note: This TOOL may be used on an individual basis or to facilitate a possible change of behavior in another person.

1. Identify a specific behavior or habit you have.

   "Every morning, before I start my work, I get a cup of coffee."

2. Build a list of payoffs or results you get from doing this behavior (see next Step). Prior to building this list you may want to know this information about payoffs.

   a. Payoffs are results you get from doing or not doing a specific behavior.

   b. Payoffs can be positive and negative, acceptable and nonacceptable, good and bad. You determine the morality of each payoff.

   c. There are numerous payoffs for each behavior.

   d. There are payoffs for everything you do or don't do.

3. Evaluate each payoff on your list by deciding whether it is positive (+) or negative (−).

165

HERE'S A CASE-IN-POINT:

Behavior: *"I drink a cup of coffee at my desk each morning before I start to work."*

Question: *"What payoffs do you get for doing this?"*

Payoffs: (+) Motivates me to get going.

(+) Stimulates my heart.

(-) Makes me nervous.

(+) Tastes good and warms my stomach.

(-) Potentially addictive.

4. Analyse the payoffs to determine if your needs are adequately being met.

   THESE QUESTIONS MAY BE HELPFUL:

   a. *"Does your current behavior give you the payoffs you want?"*
      (If you say *"Yes,"* then keep doing what you're doing.)

   b. *"If your current behavior does not give you satisfactory payoffs, what kind of substitute behavior would give you better payoffs?"*

      — Begin to identify new behaviors; get help from friends, supervisors, co-workers or books. You may want to spend time in reflection.

      — Build a list of payoffs using the above sources as helpers. Also, repeat Step #3.

      — Decide to do or not to do the new behavior. If you decide to change your behavior, use lots of reinforcement. (Reminder cards, notes, and signs are good reinforcers.)

5. If you are facilitating this process with another person, contract with this person to monitor, review and compliment any successes; also critique any failures. This reinforcement process is essential to modifying their behavior.

SITUATIONS:

- Getting your wants and needs satisfied.
- Counseling someone to see things realistically.
- Selling a product or service to a potential client.
- Helping an employee to change his or her work performance.
- Coping with a difficult situation.
- Identifying obstacles which impede a person's emotional development.
- Negotiating from a *payoff* base.
- Changing an unhealthy situation in yourself or in another.
- Motivating others to do what they need to do.
- Reinforcing healthy behaviors.

BENEFITS AND PAYOFFS:

1. Equips you with a tool for *understanding* the source of *behavior* in yourself and others.

2. Gives you opportunities to identify personal, power motivators in others.

3. Allows you to work with *difficult* people in a challenging way that meets their needs and yours.

4. Tunes you into the wavelengths of other people.

5. Stops you from wasting time and money on efforts which produce minimal results. Once you start asking people what motivates them, *you're on their right track — and yours, too!*

6. Increases your profits and quality of service. Self-motivated people are self-directed people!

7. Helps you put people "in touch" with themselves while providing them with tools to take control of their lives.

8. Makes you aware of why you do what you don't want to do, and why you do what you decide to do — for positive or negative reasons.

EXAMPLES OF PEOPLE USING THIS TOOL:

BUSINESS SETTING

(An employee makes personal phone calls during work hours. The employee and her supervisor are working together to improve this situation. Both parties build the "payoff" list, although the employee has *final say* whether or not a suggested payoff is really a payoff for her.)

PAYOFFS

(+) Convenient.

(+) Keeps me from getting bored.

(+) Keeps me "in touch" with my friends.

(-) Can't concentrate on my work.

(-) Bothers other workers near my desk.

(-) Provides an opportunity for my supervisor to give me negative feedback.

(+) Makes me look busy.

(-) Goes against company policy.

(-) *Makes me lose money as my paycheck will reflect time spent on personal business.*

The last payoff motivates the employee to change her behavior. The supervisor will work with her. The supervisor will use Step #4 and Step #5 in HOW THIS TOOL WORKS Section.

CAUTION:

DON'T try to change other peoples' behavior by building *your list of payoffs for them*.

Reason: Many people tend to support what they help create — not what you create for them. Usually, people need to build their own list of payoffs, analyze them, and decide if they are satisfied with them. If they are not satisfied with them, they may want to search for different payoffs.

DO become a change agent for *interested people*, and *show them how to build their list of payoffs* to accompany their new behaviors. If they ask you for suggestions of payoffs, give them.

TROUBLESHOOTING:

"I'm using this tool and it doesn't seem to work for me."

NATURE OF DIFFICULTY — Problem

"My department director likes to bypass other department directors when delegating jobs to certain staff members. My boss says he likes to deal directly with the staff member to insure accurate communication.

I've helped him to see that his managerial behavior has *certain payoffs* attached to it, and some of these payoffs are negative as seen by two directors. However, my boss wants to continue with his same behavior. Any suggestions?"

SUGGESTIONS:

A. Ask the other two directors to make a list of payoffs they get from reacting to your boss's behavior. Help them with this list if they ask you for suggestions. They probably will!

The directors may discover, by looking over their list, that they get other payoffs that seem to outweigh the bad ones. They may decide to accept your boss's behavior.

B. Arrange a meeting between your boss and the other two directors and let them talk about their payoffs in front of each other. A meeting of minds may occur. You need to act as a change agent during this meeting. Simply review each Step of this Tool.

C. The two directors may come up with *substitute behaviors* if your boss continues to bypass them when he delegates.

Substitute Behavior

Both directors will need to make the following request of their staffs.

When receiving work from people outside the department, please inform your immediate supervisor or director.

When conflicts in work priority occur, staff members and their immediate supervisor will resolve the matter.

> **NOTE:** PAYOFFS COME WITH EVERYTHING WE DO OR DON'T DO. MANY PEOPLE THINK THAT PAYOFFS ONLY ACCOMPANY GOOD ACTIONS. THIS IS NOT TRUE! PAYOFFS COME WITH EVERY ACTION. PAYOFFS ARE NEUTRAL AND WE MAKE THEM — GOOD — BAD — TOLERABLE — INTOLERABLE — POSITIVE OR NEGATIVE. FACE THE TRUTH! PAYOFFS ARE OUR MOTIVATORS! THIS IS A **TRADE SECRET**.

TOOL 25

VISUALIZING RESULTS

DEFINITION:

A TOOL OF THE MIND (RIGHT BRAIN THINKING) WHICH HELPS A PERSON SEE PICTURES AND OUTCOMES OF SITUATIONS AS HE OR SHE WOULD WANT THEM TO OCCUR FOR SUCCESSFUL RESULTS.

HOW THIS TOOL WORKS:

1. Learn to *fast-pace* the time of the actual event you want to visualize.

   For example, spend about 5-7 minutes visualizing yourself in the event.

2. Put yourself into a relaxed *state of body and mind*.

   HERE'S HOW TO DO IT:

   a. Close your eyes.

   b. Focus your "inner eyes" on a large, blank screen.

   c. Sit comfortably.

   d. Take a few deep breaths.

3. Program your visualization of what you want to happen.

   HERE'S THE APPROACH TO USE:

   a. See yourself as you want to be during the actual event. Project this vivid image on your blank screen.

   b. Create the coming event with as many real details as possible. Be precise with environmental details.

   — Who is present?
   — Are you sitting or standing?
   — Any distractions? How are you coping?

c. Picture your desired objectives as attained.
   — See yourself smiling and well pleased with the results.
   — Hear words of, *"Well done,"* coming from others.
   — Feel good about what you have done!

d. Now, review the entire event by focusing your attention on the process.
   — See yourself listening, speaking and handling each question with confidence.
   — See yourself coping well with conflicting views.

e. Go over the details several times as you are building memory traces for prompt recall when the actual event happens.

4. Believe in your visualizations. They will occur.

HERE'S HOW TO DO IT:

a. Hold the visualization in your mind.

b. Affirm it many times prior to the actual event.

c. See it as done, and you did it.

5. Open your eyes. You have just visualized yourself achieving successful results.

SITUATIONS:
   • Teaching yourself a skill: golf, tennis, positive thinking, etc.
   • Rehearsing a coming event: appointment, staff meeting, dinner party, etc.
   • Creating better circumstances in your life.
   • Conquering fears and other phobias.
   • Healing — in a particular area.
   • Assisting persons who interview for jobs.
   • Producing higher sales volume.
   • Dealing with problems in family relationships.
   • Striving for weight loss.
   • Changing one's thinking from "can't" to "can."

BENEFITS AND PAYOFFS:

1. Improves your capability to see better ways of coping in difficult situations.

2. Helps you crystalize your thinking and helps you acquire goal-setting skills.

3. Enables you to deal from a position of confidence because you have control of the event.

4. Exercises your intuitive and creative mind for successful outcomes. (Einstein said most of us use less than 10% of our potential. He could have been referring to the potential in our right brain.)

5. Eliminates self-induced "dis-ease."

6. Teaches you a procedure for resisting negative thoughts while encouraging you to think positively.

7. Stimulates you to create your own reality.

8. Contributes to your growth potential by having you visualize your "wants."

9. Empowers you to be a *possibility thinker.*

EXAMPLES OF PEOPLE USING THIS TOOL:

SCHEDULED EVENT: Making a Presentation

(Hal visualizes his presentation. Here is his complete visualization.)

"I see myself looking relaxed, happy and in control. I am standing at the end of the table. I feel good, prepared, and able to handle the group. Everything is in place, and so is everyone.

* * *

I picture the end results as successfully accomplished.

I made my points and answered all questions well.

I know the group is receptive to my ideas and this was my goal. I achieved it! I'm smiling on the inside, and it shows on my face. Joe just told me he was leaning toward buying my product. Great!

* * *

I rehearse the entire presentation.

I begin by welcoming the group, and setting the stage for selling my product to them. I vividly present each feature and benefit, and I show them the value of owning the product. I go over my notes in my mind's eye.

* * *

I believe in what I want and I visualize it occurring.

I believe in my ability to sell my product to this group. I believe that they will buy.

* * *

I will repeat this visualization several times to build memory traces in my mind.

I will rehearse this visualization, twice a day, until the actual presentation day."

CAUTION:

DON'T confuse Fantasizing with Visualizing. They are different functions which occur within the mind. Yet, many persons think they are visualizing when they are really fantasizing.

Reason: When people visualize, they program specific, achievable goals or objectives, and believe their goals will be accomplished. They make a commitment to get their goals achieved, and they work to achieve them. They become responsible for making their goals happen by the way they behave.

When people fantasize, they place their goal accomplishments in the hands of someone else. These people believe in impossible goals, and take little or no responsibility in seeing their goals happen. Such dreams seem magical and other-world-oriented! Fantasies do not create new realities whereas visualizations do!

Example of a Fantasy

Barry fantasizes that one year from now he will be piloting a commercial jet for a major airline company. Presently, Barry travels by air, but is not involved in Ground School or private lessons. (This is an impossible goal even for a pilot of small aircraft!)

DO learn to use the energy potential of your intuitive mind by programming visualizations which will release creative realities (goals) for you. Visualizing can give you insights and help shape your imagination. Just be clear about what you *really* want to do with your mind and then go ahead and do it.

TROUBLESHOOTING:

"I'm using this tool and it doesn't seem to work for me."

NATURE OF DIFFICULTY — Problem

"When I visualize my staff meeting starting on time, it never turns out the way I visualize it. It always starts late, and it's my meeting. What am I doing wrong?"

SUGGESTIONS:

A. For visualizations to work, you need to *really* believe in what you want to happen. You need to become assertive and announce the meeting start-up time by memo. At the scheduled time, simply begin your meeting, regardless of those coming late. (See TIME CONTRACTING TOOL, page 149, and LEGITIMIZING A MEMBER'S PRESENCE OR ABSENCE TOOL, page 109, for help.)

B. See the CAUTION Section, page 174, to be certain you are visualizing, and not fantasizing, on this event. In visualization, you must take responsibility to make the meeting occur "on time."

C. Review the Steps in this Tool on page 171. You're in for a big surprise.

NOTE: MANY CENTURIES AGO, A ROMAN STATESMAN NAMED MARCUS AURELIUS IS QUOTED AS SAYING:

> "Your life is what your thoughts make it. If you can change your thoughts, you can change your life.

YOU CAN CHANGE YOUR THOUGHTS! YOU CAN BE A POSITIVE THINKER. VISUALIZE THIS IMAGE FOR YOURSELF. IT WORKS IF YOU WORK IT. IT'S A **TRADE SECRET**!

Section II

25 REINFORCEMENT CARDS

REINFORCEMENT CARD
TOOL 1
ACTIVE LISTENING

What is it?

A Tool I use to "tune in" to the feelings and facts of the speaker so that I reflect these feelings and facts to the speaker and he or she feels understood and valued.

How do I use this Tool?

1. I listen for clues requiring active listening.
2. I keep eye contact, an open mind and a comfortable, "mirroring" posture.
3. I share "feeling words" which accurately reflect what the person is feeling.
4. I know I'm active listening when the person verifies that what I have said is a true reflection of how he or she feels.
5. I watch for clues to continue, to take another approach or to stop.

Why do I need to use this Tool?

- I believe if I listen more actively to what people are saying to me, I will be more understanding of their difficult situations.

Caution:

DON'T use active listening in all situations! Watch and listen for specific clues. When they are present, sit in your "reflective chair" and "go to work."

REINFORCEMENT CARD
TOOL 2
ASKING OPEN-ENDED QUESTIONS

What is it?

A Tool I use when I need to get information, greater clarity, more details or direct answers from speakers.

How do I use this Tool?

1. I listen to what someone is saying or I ask a question because I need more data.
2. I select stem words that reflect an open mind. "What," "When," "Why," "How," "Describe . . ," "Do . . ,"
3. I frame a "You" oriented question. *"What suggestions can you make?"*
4. I use the person's name at the beginning or at the end of my question. *"Jo, what suggestions . . ."*
5. I use eye contact and I keep my mind open.

Why do I need to use this Tool?

- I know most people like to be asked questions by people who convey a caring, non-threatening attitude in their tones.
- I receive, at times, incomplete data and I need to ask a certain type of question to get the complete data.

Caution:

DON'T ask a person too many questions at one time. Some people feel they are being manipulated and they refuse to honestly respond.

REINFORCEMENT CARD
TOOL 3
BEING ASSERTIVE AND PROACTIVE

What is it?

A Tool I use when I want to tell others my views, my beliefs, my needs or my way of doing things. In these situations, I am tactful, firm and respectful of the rights of others.

How do I use this Tool?

1. I decide to act assertively or proactively.
2. I speak or write my thoughts. I own my needs and feelings by using the pronoun "I" when necessary.
3. I select words and phrases reflecting this assertiveness. *"I need . . ," "I prefer . . ."*
4. I realize that others may view my proactive behavior differently from what I intend.
5. I do not intend to violate the other by what I say.

Why do I need to use this Tool?

- I believe in honest, direct, sensitive communication.

Caution:

DON'T allow yourself to use self-limiting behaviors such as: low tones, put downs or poor eye contact. Instead, speak up, compliment yourself and look at others.

TOOL 3

BEING ASSERTIVE AND PROACTIVE

- -

TOOL 2

ASKING OPEN-ENDED QUESTIONS

- -

TOOL 1

ACTIVE LISTENING

REINFORCEMENT CARD
TOOL 4
BUILDING POSITIVE MORALE

What is it?

A Tool I use to improve an environment by encouraging people to use certain tools on a consistent basis.

How do I use this Tool?

1. I assess my working environment and decide that improvements need to be made.
2. I select certain interpersonal tools using one tool per month. I encourage others to do the same.
3. I select a different person each month to act as my "monitor." This person critiques my use of the tool.
4. I select a "tangible reminder device" to reinforce my use of the tool. This device could change each month.
5. I schedule a review meeting every two weeks to check my progress.
6. I encourage and monitor the use of this approach with my staff.

Why do I need to use this Tool?

- I know I produce better results when my morale is positive. I know people produce better results when their morale is positive.

Caution:

DON'T give "lip service" to the idea of building positive morale. Most people detect false commitment! Once you start the process, monitor your progress and the progress of others.

REINFORCEMENT CARD
TOOL 5
CONTROLLING PERSONAL FEELINGS

What is it?

A Tool I use to get in touch with my feelings while learning how to control or regain control of them through a scheduling process.

How do I use this Tool?

1. I get in touch with the way I'm now feeling.
2. I figure out if I am consciously choosing this feeling or if I can blame someone else for making me feel this way.
3. I decide to feel this way *or* to change the way I'm feeling.
4. If I do the choosing and I want to keep the feeling, I do!
5. If I do the choosing and I want to change it, I use self-talk.
6. If I allowed someone to choose the way I feel and I want to regain my power to choose, I use self-talk and I follow the directions in Step #5.

Why do I need to use this Tool?

- I want to know how to cope with my feelings.
- I want to get rid of my blaming attitude.

Caution:

DON'T fool yourself into thinking this is easy! Habits are difficult to break — but they can be broken. Begin to talk to yourself about the way you feel. Then, take charge.

REINFORCEMENT CARD
TOOL 6
COPING WITH DIFFERENT OPINIONS

What is it?

A Tool I use to help me understand another's opinion when I don't feel the same way that he or she does. With this approach, I continue listening, with an open mind, to the person.

How do I use this Tool?

1. I listen with an open mind. Open mind = full attention.
2. I realize this person holds a different opinion.
3. I tell myself it's okay for this person to think differently from the way I do.
4. I tell the person I see it differently. I accept the fact that we think differently.
5. I build an understanding for what the other is saying by asking questions and restating, when necessary.
6. I use nonverbals (eye contact, nods of my head) and verbals to let the other know I understand his views.

Why do I need to use this Tool?

- I know how to listen to a different opinion without feeling that I have to convince the other to change to my way of thinking.

Caution:

DON'T pretend to empathize with someone whose views you do not understand. Pretense is dishonesty! Instead, make a self-disclosure statement saying that you have difficulty understanding what you are hearing.

TOOL 6
COPING WITH DIFFERENT OPINIONS

- -

TOOL 5
CONTROLLING PERSONAL FEELINGS

- -

TOOL 4
BUILDING POSITIVE MORALE

REINFORCEMENT CARD
TOOL 7
CREDITING

What is it?

A Tool I use to give "credit" to a person who deserves it.

How do I use this Tool?

1. I observe something that the person does or I hear something that the person says.
2. I write a positive comment on the person's project sheet or I tell the person that I like a specific part of his or her work.
3. I begin by using the person's name. Then, I use one of these phrases: *"John, I like," "Vivien, I reviewed ..." "Art, I want ..." "Deb, I feel ..."*
4. I touch the person by a physical gesture (touch on the arm or handshake), or by a positive look of my eye.
5. I pause to let the other person absorb my positive comment.

Why do I need to use this Tool?

- I know it makes me feel good to give credit and to get credit.
- I know other people like to receive credit too.
- Most people do better work when they feel good.

Caution:
DON'T standardize credit! Give credit consistently yet spontaneously. Pick various times and various ways of giving "credit" when and where it is due.

REINFORCEMENT CARD
TOOL 8
DECISION OWNERSHIP

What is it?

A Tool I use when I receive decisions in which I have been part of or have not been part of the decision making process.

How do I use this Tool?

1. I develop an understanding of the decision when I hear it or read it.
2. I ask questions about its source, its rationale, its parameters and its implementation.
3. When appropriate, I restate the data for better understanding.
4. I don't have to agree with the decision to understand it.
5. I own and support the decision to the best of my ability.
6. I use expressions which indicate this ownership.

Why do I need to use this Tool?

- I believe that owning decisions makes me accountable for their results.
- I do not believe in "passing the buck" when I have to implement decisions I don't like.
- I am a team member! I am responsible for what I do and for what I am asked to do.

Caution:
DON'T use other peoples' names to pass on difficult decisions. Your listeners know what you are doing and they're liable to tag you a "Buck Passer." So, use your name or the personal pronouns "I" or "We."

REINFORCEMENT CARD
TOOL 9
DEFOGGING

What is it?

A Tool I use to get precise, direct data from a person who has that data.

How do I use this Tool?

1. I listen to what the speaker is saying to me.
2. I decide that the comment represents fogging.
3. I begin to defog.
4. I ask clarifying, direct questions to "clear the air."
5. I wait for the person's response after each question.
6. When I do not understand the person's response, I make a self-disclosure statement which says, *"I don't understand your last comment. I need more clarity. Help me out."*
7. When the response is clear, specific and direct, I stop.

Why do I need to use this Tool?

- I know defogging keeps people accountable.
- I need accurate "up-to-date" information
- I believe in being proactive and direct with people.

Caution:
DON'T use sarcastic tones or aggressive talk with foggers. Some foggers don't realize what they are doing. So, use clarifying questions, assertive tones and self-disclosure statements These tools work!

TOOL 9

DEFOGGING

- -

TOOL 8

DECISION OWNERSHIP

- -

TOOL 7

CREDITING

REINFORCEMENT CARD
TOOL 10
DELEGATING

What is it?
A Tool I use when I need to tap resourceful people to get a job done effectively and efficiently.

How do I use this Tool?
1. I identify the job that needs to be delegated.
2. I select a capable and resourceful person.
3. I explain the rationale, parameters and intended results of the job I need done.
4. I give a degree of authority to the delegatee.
5. I arrange a reporting session or a completion date for monitoring purposes.
6. I ask the delegatee to restate the assignment for accuracy and mutual understanding.
7. I document, by memo, the initial delegation details.

Why do I need to use this Tool?
- I want to accomplish my work-oriented goals.
- I believe in sharing my authority through delegation.
- I need to "track" what I delegate so I can be held accountable for work slippage.

Caution:
DON'T dump or unload your undesirable work on others and call it delegating. When you delegate, give yourself sufficient time to explain the delegation in results-oriented words. Your delegatee deserves your best approach!

REINFORCEMENT CARD
TOOL 11
EYE POWER

What is it?
A Tool I use when I am listening to or speaking with people.

How do I use this Tool?
1. I listen with my eyes and my ears.
2. I focus my eyes on the eyes of the other person.
3. I do not stare or glare at the person. Every few seconds, I look away and then I look back into the eyes of the person or persons.
4. I learn to watch eye shifts and I become aware of what these eye shifts may reveal.

Why do I need to use this Tool?
- I know that listening with my eyes increases my attention span.
- I know that eyes transmit more influential power than spoken words.
- I know that listeners get more "complete messages" when they see what the speaker is saying.
- I know that speakers send better messages when they watch the other person's eyes while they speak.

Caution:
DON'T stare at people and call it "listening with your eyes." Staring tends to make people uneasy! So, from time to time, deflect your eyes away from the speaker's eyes. This can become a normal procedure. It's called "listening with your eyes and your ears!"

REINFORCEMENT CARD
TOOL 12
FOGGING

What is it?
A Tool I use when I am not willing to reveal to someone all the information I know on a given issue.

How do I use this Tool?
1. I listen to what someone is asking of me.
2. I determine how much data I want to reveal.
3. I decide to use a "fogging expression" as my response.
4. I continue to "fog" as long as it works!
5. I need to be certain that what I say is true. I don't have to tell all the truth all the time.

Why do I need to use this Tool?
- At times, I don't have the specific answers to what someone is asking for. So, I'd rather be noncommittal and give general answers.
- At times, I need to send a message to the questioner indicating some attention is being given to the request.
- When I'm in a bind, fogging gives me a way to respond.

Caution:
DON'T use fogging responses when your situation demands direct answers. In some situations, you'll need to give precise answers. So, give them!

TOOL 12

FOGGING

- -

TOOL 11

EYE POWER

- -

TOOL 10

DELEGATING

REINFORCEMENT CARD
TOOL 13
GIVING FEEDBACK

What is it?
A Tool I use when I need to give some evaluative input to a person or a group of persons concerning something they are doing.

How do I use this Tool?
1. I consider my reason for wanting to give feedback.
2. I consider the readiness of the person to receive it.
3. I use the person's name followed by the pronoun *"I."*
4. I use a verb to express what I'm about to say.
   "John, I need..." "Vivien, I reviewed..."
5. I ask the person if he or she would like to hear what I have to say. If the answer is *"No,"* I do not give it. If the answer is *"Yes,"* I continue.
6. I focus my comments on observed behavior.
7. I ask for a restatement.
8. We work out a solution together.

Why do I need to use this Tool?
- I know that avoiding a difficult situation is not the answer; confrontation is a better approach.

Caution:
DON'T fall into the trap of using the pronoun *"We"* when giving your feedback. It's better to own your feedback. So, use the pronoun *"I"* and be responsible for what you say.

REINFORCEMENT CARD
TOOL 14
HOOK QUESTIONS

What is it?
A Tool I use to persuade a person to say *"Yes"* to my questions.

How do I use this Tool?
1. I begin with a hook phrase such as: *"Don't you think..."*
2. I state my opinion on a specific issue. *"Don't you think that apples are good to eat?"*
3. I use a questioning tone.
4. I pause and wait till the person says, *"Yes."*
5. **Option:** I can state my opinion. Then, attach the hook phrase at the end of my opinion. *"I think apples are good to eat, don't you?"*

Why do I need to use this Tool?
- I like getting *"Yes"* answers to some of my questions.
- I believe in getting people to think positively.
- I like to hear support for my opinions.

Caution:
DON'T use Hook Questions indiscreetly! Some people feel manipulated when you ask them Hook or Loaded Questions. Ask a Hook Question when you want to influence the listener to hear and support your point of view.

REINFORCEMENT CARD
TOOL 15
INNER POWER

What is it?
A Tool I use to release positive energy from my inner self for personal payoffs.

How do I use this Tool?
1. I admit that I am ready to work with both parts of my mind.
2. I begin to program my subconscious when I am feeling very relaxed. I do this by myself!
3. I direct my subconscious to work out my plan or problem.
4. I do as much "groundwork" as needed.
5. I reinforce my request often. I make affirmations aloud or in writing. My conscious mind is supporting the work.
6. I withdraw my attention and let my subconscious work. My answer will come in a method or in the actual solution.
7. I evaluate my answer with my conscious mind. I use the answer or I choose not to use it.

Why do I need to use this Tool?
- I have untapped potential that needs to be activated.
- I possess positive energy for coping with my stress.

Caution:
DON'T send "mixed messages" to your subconscious and expect to receive clear answers. Your subconscious works only on what you give it. Clear instructions produce clear results.

TOOL 15

INNER POWER

- -

TOOL 14

HOOK QUESTIONS

- -

TOOL 13

GIVING FEEDBACK

REINFORCEMENT CARD
TOOL 16
LEGITIMIZING A MEMBER'S PRESENCE OR ABSENCE AT MEETINGS

What is it?
A Tool I use to acknowledge who is supposed to be at my meeting, who will be late, who will not be attending and the reasons for their absences.

How do I use this Tool?
1. I acknowledge the presence of all members. New members to the group share their name and function.
2. I acknowledge the late-arriving members, prior to their arrival, and give reasons for their delays.
3. I acknowledge the absences of any members and give reasons for their absences.
4. I ask present members to help me with reasons why certain members are absent when I have not been previously informed.
5. I use this tool at the start-up of my meeting. It takes about 10 seconds to use this tool.

Why do I need to use this Tool?
- I believe attendees have a right to know the membership of meetings and reasons why some members are not present.

Caution:
DON'T assume that attendees "could care less" why other invited members are not at the meeting. Allow your attendees access to information that is rightfully theirs!

REINFORCEMENT CARD
TOOL 17
MANAGING AND RESOLVING PROBLEMS

What is it?
A Tool I use to help other people identify, confront, manage or resolve their problems.

How do I use this Tool?
1. I need to arrange a meeting with the involved parties and discuss problem ownership principles.
2. When ownership is determined, I develop problem parameters by asking questions.
3. I need the involved parties to restate what they hear each other saying. This needs to happen frequently.
4. I allow the parties to suggest ways to solve their problem.
5. I allow the parties to select their best option for managing or resolving their problem.
6. Each party formulates an Action Plan.

Why do I need to use this Tool?
- I believe most people want to resolve their problems and some people need a third party to help them.
- I believe unattended problems become bigger problems and cause poor morale.
- I am an advocate of genuine confrontation; I am an adversary of procrastination.

Caution:
DON'T expect people to easily admit ownership of their problems. Many people tend to place blame for their problems on others. So, help those who wish to be helped!

REINFORCEMENT CARD
TOOL 18
NAME CALLING

What is it?
A Tool I use to help me remember people's names for as long as I want to.

How do I use this Tool?
1. I listen, with full attention, to the person's name.
2. I immediately say the name aloud.
3. I repeat the name silently to myself at least twice.
4. When I forget a name, I simply ask the person this question,
"What is your name? I have forgotten it."

Why do I need to use this Tool?
- I know everyone has a name and when I am talking with a person, I want to be able to use his or her name.
- I know most people like to hear their name. It's a way of giving recognition.
- I believe calling a person by name demonstrates a caring attitude.
- I send more power with my message when I direct my message to a specific person.

Caution:
DON'T overuse the other person's name. As you talk with a person, use his or her preferred name appropriately.

TOOL 18
NAME CALLING

TOOL 17
MANAGING AND RESOLVING PROBLEMS

TOOL 16
LEGITIMIZING A MEMBER'S
PRESENCE OR ABSENCE AT MEETINGS

REINFORCEMENT CARD
TOOL 19
PARAPHRASING OR RESTATING

What is it?

A Tool I use when I want to check the accuracy of my listening or speaking abilities.

How do I use this Tool?

1. I listen to the speaker's *intended message.*
2. I restate, in my own words, what I heard the speaker say.
3. I wait for some signal from the speaker that says I got the *intended message.*
4. When I get only part of the message, I ask the speaker to repeat the part I missed. Then I paraphrase it, to the speaker's satisfaction.
5. As a speaker, I can ask the listener to restate my message so that I know I'm speaking clearly.

Why do I need to use this Tool?

- I believe that listening with full attention is difficult, so I want to check what I'm hearing.
- I want to reduce the number of misunderstandings occurring in the speaking and listening process.

Caution:

DON'T psychoanalyze why the speaker feels or thinks the way he or she does. This is not paraphrasing! When you paraphrase, you restate the person's ideas without injecting any of your own ideas. Your probing questions can follow your restatement.

REINFORCEMENT CARD
TOOL 20
POSITIVE DISCIPLINING

What is it?

A Tool I use to improve the work performance of a person.

How do I use this Tool?

1. I *determine* the cause of the unacceptable work behavior.
2. I *ask* for the person's help in resolving my problem.
3. I *describe,* in detail, the unacceptable work behavior.
4. I *ask* for and initiate some steps to begin the process of resolving my problem.
5. We *decide,* by consensus, which new behavior will be practiced. We document this decision.
6. I *arrange* for informal, continual feedback sessions for checking progress. I reward and reinforce positive, acceptable behaviors.

Why do I need to use this Tool?

- I know people need to be told how to improve some of their unacceptable work behaviors.
- I believe genuine confrontation builds a person's self-esteem.

Caution:

DON'T let a person's initial resistance deter you from giving positive discipline when it's needed. Just be certain you are using this tool properly.

REINFORCEMENT CARD
TOOL 21
PROBLEM OWNERSHIP

What is it?

A Tool I use to identify and own problems that are mine and a Tool I use to help others identify and own their problems.

How do I use this Tool?

1. I determine that the situation is problematic.
2. I decide to analyze whose problem it is.
3. I ask myself if I am bothered by the situation or feeling "pinched" to the degree that it is my problem.
4. If I answer *"Yes"* to Step #3, I own the problem. Then, I determine whether my problem is one-way or two-way.
5. I use verbal/written expressions to inform others of my or our problem.

Why do I need to use this Tool?

- I believe a problem must be owned in order for a problem to exist.
- If I own a problem that is mine, I will solve or manage it differently than if I see the problem as somebody else's.

Caution:

DON'T send "You-messages" when helping people identify their problems. For instance, *"you have a problem and you need to do something about it."* If a person asks you for help in identifying problem sources, give it by using Steps #3 and #4. Also refer to the *Problem Identification Form,* page 148.

TOOL 21
PROBLEM OWNERSHIP

TOOL 20
POSITIVE DISCIPLINING

TOOL 19
PARAPHRASING OR RESTATING

REINFORCEMENT CARD
TOOL 22
TIME CONTRACTING

What is it?
A Tool I use to help me manage my time when scheduling appointments and meetings I conduct or attend.

How do I use this Tool?
1. I set up my appointments and meetings with a beginning and an end-time.
2. I negotiate for more time, when needed.
3. I will have someone remind me five minutes before the end-time of my meeting.
4. When I attend a meeting with no set end-time, I ask for one.
5. When I attend a meeting, I will remind the chairperson of his or her five minute signal.

Why do I need to use this Tool?
- I know people have things to do after my meetings and appointments.
- I, as an attendee, have a right to know how long a meeting will last. So, I will ask.
- I believe that most people don't know how to set end-times.

Caution:
DON'T develop a habit of stating end-times in approximate time frames like: *"Have you a minute?"* Too many people have too many meanings to *"a minute."* So, be precise!

REINFORCEMENT CARD
TOOL 23
UNDERSTANDING
AGREEMENT OR DISAGREEMENT

What is it?
A Tool I use to build adequate understanding without requiring others to agree or disagree with me.

How do I use this Tool?
1. I listen with an open mind to the speaker(s).
2. I ask questions or paraphrase to gain a deeper understanding.
3. I know that understanding doesn't require me to agree or disagree with the other person.
4. When I understand, I tell the other person.
5. I am free to add, *"I agree"* or *"I disagree."*
6. I avoid using the expression, *"Do you understand,"* when I speak with others.

Why do I need to use this Tool?
- I believe in building understanding instead of assuming understanding.
- I believe people have a right to know when I understand what they are saying.
- I know I can give commitment and support once I understand.

Caution:
DON'T use trite expressions like: *"Have you got that?"* or *"Ok?"* If you want to check the listener's ability to understand you, ask him or her to paraphrase your comments.

REINFORCEMENT CARD
TOOL 24
USING MOTIVATORS AND PAYOFFS

What is it?
A Tool I use to help some people know why they do what they do or why they don't do what they're supposed to do. I can use this Tool on myself too!

How do I use this Tool?
1. I pick out a specific behavior or habit I have or someone else has.
2. I list payoffs I get for keeping this habit. Others can do the same.
3. I evaluate each payoff as a positive or negative one. Others check their lists too.
4. I assess each payoff to determine if it helps or hinders me in satisfying my wants or needs. The other person does the same.
5. I'm aware that "payoffs" motivate. Others know this too. So, we choose to improve, change or remain with the same habit.
6. If I, or the other person, decide to improve or change, we will need support.

Why do I need to use this Tool?
- I know I do what I do because of the payoffs I get. Different payoffs require changes in my behavior. Other people operate the same way.

Caution:
DON'T build another person's list of payoffs. People tend to support what they help create, not what you create for them. You can help.

TOOL 24

USING MOTIVATORS AND PAYOFFS

- -

TOOL 23

UNDERSTANDING
AGREEMENT OR DISAGREEMENT

- -

TOOL 22

TIME CONTRACTING

REINFORCEMENT CARD
TOOL 25
VISUALIZING RESULTS

What is it?

A Tool I use to help my mind *see* pictures and outcomes of situations as I would *want* them to be.

How do I use this Tool?

1. I learn to fast-pace the future situation as I would want it to be.
2. I relax, close my eyes and begin to visualize what I want to happen.
3. I *see* my intended objectives being achieved.
4. I *see* myself interacting with certain people and I *see* myself handling each interaction with ease.
5. I review the process several times and each time, I *see* my objectives being achieved.
6. I believe that what I have visualized will occur.

Why do I need to use this Tool?

- I need to creatively plan my meetings instead of allowing them to happen and hoping for good results.
- I need to deal from a position of confidence. Visualizing will give me this positional power.

Caution:

DON'T confuse Fantasizing with Visualizing! Fantasizing deals with impossible and unrealistic goals. Visualizing deals with achievable goals, and you work to make them happen.

TOOL 25

VISUALIZING RESULTS

- -

ABOUT THE AUTHOR

MARTHA LANGDON-DAHM, Ph.D. is President and Co-Founder of LEARNING DEVELOPMENT SYSTEMS, INC., a training, consulting and publishing firm specializing in personnel development and management education.

She received her Ph.D. in Organizational Behavior from The Union Graduate School. As a professional educator, Dr. Langdon-Dahm has more than twenty years' experience in organizational behavior and human resource development.

Dr. Langdon-Dahm has consulted and conducted training programs for the United States Office of Personnel Management, the U.S. Air Force, the U.S. Navy, the Defense Logistics Services, Fortune 500 companies, the United Way of America, universities and other educational institutions. She has designed and facilitated hundreds of workshops and seminars for managers, supervisors, and nonsupervisory employees.

In addition, Dr. Langdon-Dahm holds membership in the American Society for Training and Development. An innovator and change agent, she has authored a manual on the effective utilization of employee resources.

Dr. Langdon-Dahm's other publications are: *Training Designs for Human Resource Development, Utilizing Staff Resources, Assertive Writing* and a Simulation Instrument on *Conflict in Organizational Settings.*